The Enchantment of Reason

The Enchantment of Reason

PIERRE SCHLAG

Duke University Press

Durham and London

1998

© 1998 Duke University Press
All rights reserved
Printed in the United States of America on acid-free paper ∞
Typeset in Carter and Cone Galliard by Tseng Information Systems, Inc.
Library of Congress Cataloging-in-Publication Data appear
on the last printed page of this book.

Contents

Acknowledgments   ix

Introduction: Following the Letter of the Law   1
The Purloined Letter   2
The Logic of the Frame   3
Two Kinds of Errors   4
Professional Solipsism   5
There's No Failure Like Success   6
Wherever You Go There You Are   8
The Object of Desire   8
The Lure of the Real   9
Comfort and Dread   10
Reason in Law   12
Itinerary   15

1   Faith in the Power of Reason   19
The Stakes   20
The Rule of Reason   22
Central Command and the Big Tent   26

2   When Reason Runs Out   30
The Noble Scam   33
Nodding Heads Agree   37
Reason Rules   38

3   The Arguments for Reason   40
The Reasonableness of Reason   41
In Praise of Reason (The Argument from Virtue)   47
The Argument from Fate   53
Reason's Raison d'Être   58

4   Predicaments of Reason   60
Belief in, for, and through Reason   61
Critical Reflexivity and Frame Construction   63
Working at a Useless Task   71
Activity and Order   76
Constitutive Vulnerabilities   78
Modesty   79
False Modesty: The Strange Case of Neopragmatism   81
Language Games about Language Games   86
Presumption   90

5   Divine Deceptions   92
Enchantment   95
The Ways of Enchantment   97
The Progressive Fallacy and the Last Laugh of Metaphysics   98
The Objectivist Aesthetic   100
The Subjectivist Aesthetic   104
The Roles of the Objectivist and the Subjectivist Aesthetic   106
"As If" Jurisprudence   108
The Transmigration of Authority   111
The Name of the Answer   112
When Reason Can't Stop Making Sense   115
From Virtual Law to Virtual Reason   119
Just the Facts   124

6   The Legal Self   126
Rationalism   127
Separating Self from Object   127
Separating Self from Context   128
Take This and Choose It   129
This Is Not a Stop Sign   131
False Empowerment   133
Free to Be Framed   135
Dominance and Submission   135

Epilogue: Reason without End   141
Boring and Dreary/Dreary and Boring   141
Nihilism   142
Life in the Grid—Running the Mazes   142

The Shallowness Problem   143
The Excessive Construction of Everything   144
Reason/Not   144

Notes   147
Index   157

Acknowledgments

Writing a book like this would not have been possible twenty-five years ago. Back then, the legal academy was only beginning to toy with the idea of "theory." Anti-theory was not on the charts. Law and economics were still embryonic. Critical legal studies had yet to be invented. Jurisprudence was busy playing out its variations on the natural law/positivism debate. Legal philosophy consisted mainly of plumbing the depths of "reflective equilibrium" and keeping up with the Warren Court.

So, until recently, writing a book like this would have been unthinkable. One result is that I am in the position of having way too many people to thank. Here is the short list.

I thank Duncan Kennedy and Stanley Fish—neither of whom have read this book—but both of whom have had a manifest intellectual influence on my work. There are others who deserve thanks. Marge Brunner, Cynthia Carter, Anne Guthrie, Linda Spiegler, Diana Stahl, and Kay Wilkie provided excellent office support. Craig Callen, Paul Campos, Rebecca French, Bob Nagel, David Skover, Steve Smith, and Alexander Somek read all or parts of this manuscript at various stages of completion and provided many helpful comments and criticisms. Here at Colorado, the intellectual companionship of Paul Campos, Rebecca French, and Steve Smith has been essential to this undertaking. Finally, the University of Colorado School of Law deserves thanks for fostering a community in which law is not simply something one thinks within, but also something one thinks about—and even, occasionally, something one thinks against.

For all this, I am grateful.

Introduction: Following the Letter of the Law

> The measures adopted were not only the best of their kind, but carried out to absolute perfection. Had the letter been deposited within the range of their search, these fellows would beyond a question, have found it. EDGAR ALLAN POE [1]

When one is enchanted by reason, it does not feel like enchantment at all. Instead, it feels quite reasonable. Suppose you were in thrall to the enchantment of reason, how would you know? What you would be experiencing could be described as an immoderate confidence, an excessive faith, in (your) reason. This immoderate confidence would translate into a kind of overextension of reason: reason and its creations would substitute for experience, emotion, empirical observation, research (and so on). You would be trying to reason your way through everything. If you were subject to such an enchantment of reason, how could you tell?

The answer is hardly obvious. Consider two possibilities.

First possibility: Perhaps you could "grok" your way to a recognition that your reasoning has become excessive, your ratiocination immoderate. But then a moment's pause. You think. You ask: "But what is the status of my groking? Does groking trump reason?" And, of course, at that point, your reason would be off and running again. . . .

Second possibility: You might be able to reason your way to a recognition that your reasoning has become excessive. But since, at that point, reason is under a cloud, it is not as if you can trust the critical deployment of your reason to adjudicate the status of your reason.

You are in deep trouble.

One way of telling that reason has run amok would be in the feedback you receive from others. But consider now the possibility that it is not simply *your* reason that has become enchanted, but the reason of your entourage—your academic discipline, your profession, your culture.

If that were the case, your excessive faith in reason would be perfectly consonant with that of your entourage. Your exigent demands for coherence and consistency would resonate with the standards of your milieu.

In these circumstances, it would be exceedingly difficult to recognize the enchantment of reason. And the reason is simple: in such circumstances, the very forces that have led to the enchantment of reason have also liquidated the intellectual and cultural resources that would allow the recognition that reason has become enchanted.

It is, of course, debatable whether—and if so, to what extent—such a scenario describes our circumstances (academic or otherwise). I will not argue the point here. (The book that follows is the argument.) Instead, in this introduction, I am concerned with a more preliminary matter. Specifically, the concern is that the enchantment of reason has become so successful—at least in some milieus—that we have already largely lost the capacity to recognize the enchantment of reason for what it is.

My concern here then is to show how reason continues to seem so well reasoned, so reasonable even as it becomes enchanted—and goes dramatically wrong. I would like to show how this enchantment of reason proceeds, how it seems plausible, and how it maintains itself. By way of illustration, I offer Edgar Allan Poe's "The Purloined Letter."

Among other things, "The Purloined Letter" is a cautionary tale about reason and the enchantment of reason. While the tale can be read in many ways,[2] its import here is to provide a graphic illustration of how and why professionals can become enchanted by their own disciplinary reason. The professionals who go wrong in "The Purloined Letter" are the police. Arguably, the very way in which the police go wrong is the way in which various academic disciplines go wrong. And for much the same reasons.

The Purloined Letter

A letter has been stolen. The letter is in the possession of the thief, a public minister. The divulgation of the letter's contents would compromise the queen. That is the letter's value—as the thief, the queen, the police, the detective, and the reader well know.

So begins Edgar Allan Poe's "The Purloined Letter." Like almost all detective stories, it is an enlightenment narrative. It is a narrative where reason is called upon to search out the truth and to resolve the mystery.

Where is the letter? The police have searched the apartments of the thief meticulously, checked for false drawers, secret compartments, and the like—all to no avail. The detective, Dupin, is consulted. He diagnoses the failure of the police. Their problem is their method. At first, this may seem odd for theirs is an extremely careful method:

> We examined the rungs of every chair in the hotel, and indeed, the jointings of every description of furniture, by the aid of the most powerful microscope. . . . [A]nd when we had absolutely completed every particle of the furniture in this way, then we examined the house itself. We divided its entire surface into compartments, which we numbered, so that none might be missed; then we scrutinized each individual square inch throughout the premises.[3]

This method is familiar to us. A subject matter is territorialized and sub-divided into a grid. The contiguous compartments are identified and subdivided in turn. The gesture is then repeated. This is the aesthetic of the map, the outline, the index, the decision tree, the flow chart, the chain of command, the hard drive, the taxonomy, the analysis, and so on. Interestingly, it is also the ruling organizational form of many contemporary academic disciplines. Some disciplines—American law comes to mind—are almost wholly given over to this taxonomic form. In such disciplines, the resulting disciplinary gridwork has become exquisitely exact—permitting extraordinarily precise conceptual calibrations.

But precision and exactitude are not everything. The police in "The Purloined Letter" learned this point the hard way: with all their care and caution, they missed the letter. The detective explains why: the methods of the police are "but an exaggeration *of the application* of the one principle or set of principles of search."[4]

But what is wrong with the *exaggeration* of the application of a set of principles? In one sense, nothing—nothing, providing that one has the *right* set of principles and that *application* is the operation called for. But there's the rub. In "The Purloined Letter," the police did not have the right set of principles. And so no matter how carefully they applied those principles, they would always miss the mark.

The way in which the police miss their mark is interesting precisely because it goes way beyond what is ordinarily considered police work. Indeed, it sheds some light on the way in which academic disciplines miss their mark.

The Logic of the Frame

How then did the police go wrong? Let us work backward. Here is how the thief "concealed" the letter: He changed its physical appearance by removing the original black seal and affixing a small red seal instead. He soiled the paper so that the letter would have the appearance of something of no particular import. Finally, he placed the letter in a card rack with other correspondence.

When the police arrive at the thief's apartment, they are, of course, in a certain frame of mind. They have expectations, desires, procedures, and protocols. They are looking for a physical object—a letter with a big black seal. They believe that the letter is hidden—that it is a hidden thing. They also believe that the letter is located within the delimited space of the thief's apartment. Given that particular framing of the problem, their grid-like search makes a great deal of sense: the object must, after all, be found within the delimited space. It is only a question of ensuring that no space is left unchecked, no volume unexamined.

Two Kinds of Errors

The police fail to turn up the letter. And while there are many ways in which one might describe the failure of the police methods, I will describe only two.

First, one could say that the police erred in the way in which they framed their search. The failure of the police was in framing a kind of search that was inappropriate for the object they sought. The logic of their search was off. Their method was like a sieve. The problem is that they deployed the wrong kind of sieve—one that let the letter fall through. This kind of framing error forms the basis for a standard antiformalist point—one that is familiar to many academic thinkers, particularly in American law. The point is: *One can only find what the search allows in the sense that the search fails to recognize anything else.*

There is a second way in which the error of the police methods can be described. This too is an antiformalist point, but it is less familiar, perhaps because more disturbing. The police fail because they have miscast the object of inquiry (the letter). They have literally misidentified their own desire. They have miscast the identity of the letter by treating it as an immutable physical object, an artifact—a piece of paper with a black seal and a bold address. In short, not only do the police search in the wrong way, but they search for the wrong thing. They are searching for something that literally does not exist. The point is: *One can only find what the search allows in the sense that the search institutes what it is one is looking for.*

Why don't the police understand these two points? It is not clear. We are not told. Perhaps it is precisely because *they are* the police. And as the police, it is not their job to understand the finer points of antiformalism.

Instead, what the police do is apply the same routine operations and procedures to each scenario regardless of context. And much of the time—on average—these operations and procedures "work." But not always.

Professional Solipsism

One of the striking aspects of the police behavior in "The Purloined Letter" is how enchanted the police become by their method when it does not yield the desired results. Rather than abandoning their search or devising some new one, they redouble their efforts and apply the same protocols and procedures, ever more rigorously.

They have lapsed into a kind of professional solipsism. What renders this professional solipsism possible is precisely the interplay of their two failures. When the police territorialize the apartment of the thief and when they cast the letter as an object with distinct physical characteristics, they are in both cases working off the same grid. They are thinking of their search and of the letter in the same objectivist aesthetic: for them, the letter is a determinate thing located in a demarcated three-dimensional space.

The irony is that no amount of calibration of their method in terms of its object (or vice versa) could possibly help the police. The logic of their search and the object of their inquiry have both been cast in the wrong frame. No amount of "reflective equilibrium" between what they seek and how they go about it could possibly help. Indeed, the logic of their search is already perfectly attuned to the object of their inquiry (and vice versa). They are searching very consistently, very coherently, very methodically in the wrong way for the wrong thing.

Ultimately, the efforts of the police must come to an end. Indeed, it is difficult to imagine that their solipsistic activities would continue indefinitely. Either they will find the letter through happenstance, or they will give up. Their search must come to an end because there really is a letter to be found. There really is—Poe has given it to us—a fact of the matter.

This is not obviously the case in contemporary academic disciplines. In the contemporary context of the social sciences, the humanities, and the law, it is not clear that there is "a letter"—a fact of the matter—to be found. The "methods" deployed by the various disciplines thus present a certain risk. The risk is not that these disciplines will fail to find their respective "letters." On the contrary, the risk is that they will find their "letters" over and over again—repeatedly, ever more precisely. The risk, in other words, is that they will find what they are searching for—even though what they are searching for is little more than the construction of the logic of their own disciplinary frames.

There's No Failure Like Success

Since, in the academic context, the object of inquiry is often a construction of the same frame that constructs the logic of the search, one would predict a certain success. One would predict that if disciplines are able to cast their *objects of inquiry* in terms of their own *logics of search* that success would be a rather frequent phenomenon.

And so, often it is: in many contemporary disciplines—American law, for instance—it seems we often have the "exaggeration of the application of a set of principles." We have the repetition of a series of methodical operations aimed at an object of inquiry that is itself a construction of the discipline.

The resemblance between the methods of the police and contemporary American academic disciplines goes even further. Many academic disciplines—again, American law is a good example—have taken on specific policing roles. Thus, not only do some disciplines mimic the obsessively repetitive methods of the police in "The Purloined Letter," but one of the methods they obsessively mimic is precisely that of policing.

The similarity does not end here. Indeed, the very kind of policing that goes on in the academy is often isomorphic with the objectivist grid thinking of the police. In the academy, there is a tremendous amount of crude thinking—often done in the name of "rigor"—that consists of evaluating any new work to make sure that it conforms to the same old grid.

Indeed, it is striking how much of intellectual life in the academy is governed by criteria that are related to the image of the grid. Consider, as examples, just three notions that are generally presumed to be essential to "good" legal thought: coherence, comprehensiveness, and determinacy. All three are notions that relate intimately to the grid. The notion that it is appropriate for legal thought to be "coherent"—in the sense of hanging well together—is a specification for a properly constructed grid: coherence requires that all the compartments be of the same kind so as to fit within the same plane. Another requirement generally widely believed in American law is that legal thought must be "comprehensive." This can be understood as another aspect of the recipe for a properly constructed grid: all the compartments must be included, none left missing. Another requirement which often goes by the name of "determinacy" also relates to the grid: it requires that the operation of subdivision be performed rigorously—that the resulting compartments be defined precisely so that there are proper conceptual boundaries separating and defining each compartment. All of these grid notions (and many others) are tacitly accepted not just in law, but in many other corners of the university as defining proper methodology.

Of course, for all its drudgery, academic police work has its place. It has its role. And it is an important role. Indeed, even in "The Purloined Letter," the detective's deductions depend upon the prior performance (and failure) of the police search. Besides, the detective is somewhat of a policeman himself—policing the police as it were. For these reasons, there can be no outright rejection of police work in intellectual pursuits. Academic policing maintains the architecture of the discipline, identifies error, excludes irrelevancies, and so on. Without disciplinary policing, very little of intellectual value is possible.

So there can be no outright rejection of police work in the academy. At the same time, however, policing itself can go wrong. And to that claim, it is no answer to say that policing polices itself. For such self-policing is of no use whatsoever, if it is itself conducted with the wrong "methods" seeking out the wrong "errors." Being careful, cautious, and rigorous is of no help whatsoever if the way in which one does any of these things is itself wrong-headed. There is no great virtue in being "rigorously" wrong. More importantly, perhaps—and this is a point that is especially relevant to the discipline of American law—there is no virtue in trying to be careful, cautious, or rigorous if there is nothing to be careful, cautious, or rigorous with. It just adds to the noise.

To put it in the terms of "The Purloined Letter," policing is only as good as the grids it deploys. And that is to say, that despite its good intentions, its rigor, and its coherence, sometimes policing will be downright awful. What is more, when policing is downright awful, it will be downright awful in a systematic way. Like the police in "The Purloined Letter," it is difficult for many contemporary academic thinkers to understand this point. The very idea that the methods, protocols, procedures of a discipline could be lacking in value is simply unthinkable to those immersed in the discipline. Such thoughts are unthinkable for much the same reasons that Poe's police would find such thoughts unthinkable.

Why do the police fail to understand the shortcoming of their methods? Why do academics? Consider the possibilities.

Wherever You Go There You Are

Consider the response of the police when their methods fail to turn up the letter. They intensify the search by repeating the same methods only with more vigor, with greater precision. It does not occur to the police that their failure is occasioned precisely by their search method. Indeed, as Stanley Fish might say, it cannot occur to them for they are already operating within their search methods and from that vantage point, the mistake occasioned by that method simply cannot be seen.[5] The same is true of disciplinary thinkers: to the extent that their thinking not only constructs the logic of their search, but the object of their inquiry, they cannot see what they are missing. Within those parameters the claim that their searches lack value simply cannot register: indeed, how could it, when the search seems, and with some regularity, to produce what it is searching for?

The Object of Desire

For the police, the object of desire is the letter. But through their "methods" they have substituted a simulacrum of the letter for the real object of their desire. Instead of the letter that they desire, they have substituted the image of the letter, a proxy, a simulacrum—specifically, a piece of paper with a big black seal. But that piece of paper is not what they truly desire. It is, instead, an image, a symptom, a symbol, an association of what they desire. What they desire is the letter, in its capacity as meaning.

This substitution of image for identity, of simulacrum for original, is not something the police notice. The fact of substitution does not occur to them. The result is that when called upon to revise or improve their search, they do so in terms of an image, a simulacrum of the object of desire. There can be all sorts of adjustments between *the logic of the search* and *the object of desire*—but all this adjustment will be for naught, because the police's understanding of the letter is a mere simulacrum, an imagistic approximation, of what they actually desire.

In academic circles, such substitutions abound. In American law, there is a great deal of work, for instance, that concerns the relation between laws (all kinds of laws) and justice (all kinds of justice). But as with the police, legal thinkers often fail to recognize that they are operating within a frame in which the object of their desire, justice, has already been replaced by "justice"—a term whose meaning and appropriate modes of use are largely a function of academic fashions, protocols, anxieties, ambitions, wish fulfillment, and other formations that often have very little relation to justice.

The problem is that, like the police, many academics seem to have no clue that such crucial substitutions may have already occurred. Many legal academics, for instance, genuinely seem to believe that when they advocate "progressive legal change" in the pages of the law reviews, they are somehow actually helping to advance progressive legal change. It seems not to have occurred to them that the net effect of their advocacy might amount to little more than the circulation of a three-word phrase—"p-r-o-g-r-e-s-s-i-v-e l-e-g-a-l c-h-a-n-g-e"—through the disciplinary grids of American legal thought. The same, of course, would be true of "e-f-f-i-c-i-e-n-c-y" or, indeed, any term that does not hook up with the already-in-place inclinations and commitments of judges and other legal actors.

If legal and other academics fail to notice that the identity of the letter has been switched on them, if they fail to notice, for instance, that advocating "progressive legal change" $\neq$ advancing progressive legal change, it is because they have fully assimilated the discipline's conflation of the two. The important point to notice is that such substitutions of image for identity or simulacrum for original are often invisible precisely because the substitutions are themselves effectuated by and throughout the discipline. Like the police, the academics settle for and settle into the pursuit of a simulacrum of the object of their desire. They once aspired to be detectives, but they ended up as (academic) traffic cops.

The Lure of the Real

There is another reason the police and the academics believe in their grids. What renders the methods of the police creditable, at least to them, is that the methods appear to be anchored in a sensate real. The apartment is real, the letter is real, the numbering is real—in the same way that physical reality is grasped as being real.[6] The dominant metaphor for the real, among the police, is space—hence the logic of the police search is cast in spatial terms: territorialization, subdivision, mapping, and compartmentalization.[7]

Strikingly, what is not a dimension of the real in their frame is time. Time is strangely absent in the police version of the real—which is why they can keep up the search for such a long time without recognizing its futility. The police search is frozen in spatial aesthetics without any consideration of time. Theirs is a static frame—which is why the very idea that objects—most notably letters—can change in identity and in appearance does not occur to them. Change is a function of time. And time is no part of their frame.

The police have, in short, a simple idea of the real. It is an appealing one, at least to them, precisely because it does not change. Their methods seem real to them, precisely because the reality of the spatial in the physical world is transposed to their protocols and procedures. The spatial metaphors and images enable the transposition of the reality of the spatial to their procedures and protocols.

The dominance of spatial aesthetics in the social sciences and the humanities works the same magic. If there is going to be an academic discipline, an enduring frame, then the effects of time must be minimized. And it is space that will serve as the dominant image and metaphor of the real.

Time will either be denied or colonized by spatial metaphors that enable the stabilization of frame. Hence it is that academic disciplines routinely invoke spatial containments of time: periodization, succession, and so on. In American law, the ruling metaphor for time is the linear function known as "progress." Hence, for instance, legal thinkers will sometimes say, "With recent advances in analytical philosophy, we can now see that . . ." The raw improbability—indeed the comical character—of such claims seems entirely to escape their authors.

And in one sense it is easy to understand why—and not just in law. The borrowing of scientific metaphors, images, and ambitions by some academic disciplines enables their practitioners to presume an almost sensate reality to the grids and operations of their own disciplines.

Comfort and Dread

There is yet a fourth reason that the police and the academics cling to their grid. To put it bluntly, it is less than pleasant to actually consider the emptiness of a discipline when it is one's own. When the same disciplinary frame institutes not only the logic of search (the methods), but the field (the apartment) and the object of inquiry (the letter), the ghost of emptiness begins to haunt the discipline. The circularity starts to wear thin.

The discipline can begin to seem somewhat solipsistic. The thought arises that it may be the sort of discipline destined to find the answers it seeks because it has already constructed the answers. This is not a pleasant thought. It is particularly unpleasant and yet particularly applicable to those disciplines that look the most like the "methods" of the police.

Understandably, few disciplinary thinkers can be counted upon to consider the emptiness of their own disciplines with great enthusiasm. The disciplinary thinkers will resist this possibility for three reasons.

First, those who, like thinkers in law, have invested hard, painful labor into the mastery of dry, obscure, and maddeningly intricate grids are unlikely to consider such a thought for very long. On the contrary, what one would expect from such thinkers is a certain *ressentiment* against those who have not experienced the dreary toiling in the disciplinary trenches. As a general matter, the more painful the mastery of a discipline was to acquire, the less its practitioners will be willing to give it up.

There is a second reason that disciplinary thinkers will fail to own up to the possibility. For disciplinary thinkers to pursue the possibility that their discipline is organized in solipsistic lines would be to relinquish the advantages that their discipline has bestowed upon them. The cost is highest among those who have been most successful. These leaders are the least likely to turn against their discipline. In American law, loyalty to the discipline is particularly alluring because the discipline is understood (however erroneously) to feed into the channels of worldly power: high government office.

There is a third, perhaps even stronger, reason that disciplinary thinkers will not consider the emptiness of their discipline. It turns out that the solipsism of the search that always finds the object it constructs is not a problem specific to any particular discipline, but rather one that is *more* or *less* common to all. If the problem is well nigh unavoidable, why then not stay with the grid that one knows rather than switch to the ones that one doesn't? Why turn against the grid?

Why not simply run the academic mazes like the police and continue the "*exaggerated application* of a principle or a set of principles"? Why not continue to polish the grid, monitor its relays, supervise its connections?

I have already hinted at some answers. The remainder of this book will elaborate.

Reason in Law

This book deals with reason in the discipline of American law. In some sense, this focus is quite parochial. The problems confronting the discipline of American law are, to a large degree, distinct from the problems presented in other disciplines.

For one thing, it is a serious question whether American law is indeed a discipline or instead an admixture of thinking habits, jargons, ideals, anxieties, and canonical materials that are reproduced with sufficient regularity (hence, "the grid") to produce the appearance of an intellectual discipline. As others have noted, it is difficult to discern precisely what the discipline of American law might be: it has no great texts, no widely accepted methods, no enduring questions of any great intellectual depth. If American law is an intellectual discipline, it is not at all clear what the content of this discipline might be.[8]

For a second thing, the discipline of American law (if I can call it that) has, from its initial formative years been committed to the rationalization of the positive law of the state (cases, statutes, constitutions). While American legal thinkers have for the most part been very critical of specific cases, statutes, constitutional provisions, and the like, they have nonetheless been very critical in a very narrow way—a way that presumes and systematically reaffirms the essential rationality and essential value of American law. The discipline of American law, from its very beginnings (and without much critical reflection), has been committed to the rationalization of official government actions that are themselves not obviously the product of reason or rationality, but also an admixture of all sorts of forces, to wit: tradition, experience, power politics, rent seeking, utopian hopes, dystopian fears, expediency, practicality.

There is a third thing that distinguishes American law from other disciplines and keeps it in a relatively backward state. The discipline of American law is protected. It enjoys state-enforced barriers to entry. And there is a very good (even if socially contingent) reason for that. "Law" *is* the language of the American liberal state. It is the language through which the state organizes itself, effectuates its actions, and legitimates itself and its actions to its subjects. The upshot is that, if there were no discipline of American law, the liberal state would have to invent it. What guarantees the effective existence of something that looks like the discipline of American law is precisely that the liberal state requires the existence of such a discipline. As far as the continued existence of the liberal state is concerned, the humanities can wither: classics, philosophy, and literature can fall into disrepair. But the discipline of American law must endure. And if the discipline of law cannot endure—if it has no "there" there—it must be faked, bluffed, or simulated.

All of this is to say that there is some basis for thinking that in American law reason is particularly compromised. The tasks that reason is called upon to perform in law are such that it may be unwise to extrapolate from the parochial character of the discipline of American law to other disciplines or to the wider culture.

At the same time, however, it might be noted that all disciplines within the university are committed to the maintenance of their own identities as disciplines. This would be true of even those most critical of disciplines which are, if nothing else, committed to the maintenance of their critical identities. To that extent, many disciplines in the humanities and in the social sciences share the same precritical commitment as law toward their own defining architecture. One would expect then that these other disciplines also advance a kind of knowledge that celebrates and glorifies their own internal architecture. Hence it is that today the modern university exhibits a contest of faculties wherein each discipline celebrates its own architecture and tries to colonize all the others. Analytical philosophers adjudicate the value of the claims made by lawyers, sociologists, and others. Sociologists reduce legal or philosophical thinking to material or social determinations (and so on and so forth). What each discipline has in common with the others is a powerful urge to lay down the law— namely, its own.

And, indeed, it is striking that when the social sciences and the humanities are not busy imitating the style of the natural sciences, they are often emulating the aesthetics of law. The aesthetics of a great deal of analytical philosophy, for instance, looks highly reminiscent of the stylistic features of a federal statute: definitions, divisions, subdivisions, cross-references—all highly formalized. The technocratic flavor of economic analysis and econometrics often displays the same characteristics—a zeal to articulate the law and the suitably specified conditions that govern given economic phenomena. The outbreak of "theory" in all domains of learning from literary criticism to anthropology can be seen itself as an outbreak of "law." Not all theory is lawlike, but a great deal of it (especially in its normative dimension) clearly is. Theory, after all, is very often a way of "laying down the law," of stating the abstract rules and regularities by which various phenomena are or should be governed.

This disciplinary drive toward regulatory formalization is obviously not the only one in the humanities and the social sciences; there are also powerful "postmodern" tendencies toward dispersion and fragmenta-tion. But, ironically, these "postmodern" tendencies create precisely the backlash leading to further regulatory formalization. There's nothing like schizophrenia to make formalism look good.

All of this is to say that the desire to "lay down the law" is not at all confined to the discipline of American law. Rather, in its desire to lay down the law, American law may well be emblematic of a plight encoun-tered in many disciplines.

It may even be symptomatic of broader tendencies throughout the greater American culture. Indeed, as American law proliferates, its aes-thetic has become epidemic in American culture. Law—in the sense of authoritative codification—has become the desired end point of all kinds of political programs from the far right to the far left. The patriot mili-tias, the Christian right, the pro-life groups, the school curricular reform movements, the pro-choice groups, the affirmative action partisans, the gay-lesbian rights groups—all speak in a legalist idiom and seek to insti-tute their politics in the aesthetics of the legal code. Politics seems to have its end in regulation. For every problem, it seems, there is a solution, and the solution is almost always law. There is thus some basis for thinking that the impulse to law, the impulse to legislate, to regulate, is cultural— much broader and much deeper than its technical formalized expression within the discipline of American law or even American positive law.

In other words, one could understand the plight of reason in American law, not so much as an oddity or a peculiarity, but rather as emblematic or symptomatic of some much broader cultural tendencies. In this sense, rather than seeing the discipline of American law as an intellectual back-water in which reason is particularly compromised, one could begin to see American law as a particularly advanced example of much broader cultural tendencies. The discipline of American law could thus be seen as a particularly disturbing image of our future: the enchantment of reason.

I leave the extrapolations unfinished. It is for others to examine to what extent the enchantment of reason in the discipline of American law is one that has also affected their domain. I will, however, for ease of reading sometimes drop the reference to "American" in reference to law and legal thought. But though I drop the adjective "American" here or there, it is important for the reader to understand that my claims con-tinue to refer to American law and American legal thought. The social and intellectual contexts in which law and legal thought is produced in other countries is likely to differ and to require a different analysis.

Meanwhile, here is the itinerary.

Itinerary

Why is reason so important to law? Why do jurists and legal thinkers consider it important to rationalize law—to show that it is rational and to cast law in the image of reason? These are the questions addressed in the first chapter, "Faith in the Power of Reason." The stakes are rather large: the reason of law not only underwrites the rule of law but provides a sense of comfort and control to jurists and citizens alike. The role played by reason is significant. Reason is the medium that unifies the field or fields of law. Reason is understood to be the medium that allows the representation of the field as connected, as hanging together—thereby allowing law to make its moves.

Here we can begin to see the structural possibility for the enchantment of reason. Reason is crucially important to "law"—it is the formative medium through which the field of law is organized and represented. The formative importance of reason sets the scene for its enchantment. Because reason is so fundamental to the way in which we think and represent our world, it is precisely the sort of thing that eludes us. We are very much without the frames to get a good grasp on its identity. Instead, we are within the field that it establishes for us (and in us). Reason—given its constitutive role—will enchant us and our law. (That particular enchantment will not reach full bloom until the fifth chapter, "Divine Deceptions.") Moreover, because reason seems to play such a crucial role, any and all kinds of forces, agendas, and programs will try to enlist reason in their own (sometimes greatly unreasoned) causes. Over time, reason becomes diffused and distorted.

In the second chapter, "When Reason Runs Out," we encounter the moment when reason is unable to furnish answers in law—when some choice must be made between X and Y and reason supports both sides. These are circumstances faced frequently by appellate and trial court judges. They are called upon to decide between distributive justice or corrective justice, written law or unwritten law, security or freedom, certainty or flexibility, and the like. What happens in these circumstances?

Here we encounter the enchantment of reason in one of its crudest and most deliberate forms. When reason runs out, everyone simply pretends that it doesn't. The self-evident, the obvious, is simply presented as if it were the work of reason itself. And the *nodding heads* agree. They nod and they say, "Yes, yes, we *here* all agree with each other; we are the voice of reason." This move is not pretty; it is often a scam, but, often enough, it works. In American law, this particular scam does a lot of work. And after a while, through sheer repetition, the nodding heads actually start to believe their own lines, "Yes, we are the voice of reason. Yes, that's it. . . . And we say that . . . Yes, and . . ."

In the third chapter, "The Arguments for Reason," I consider the claims made by various self-announced "partisans of reason," such as Professors Cass Sunstein and Martha Nussbaum, who try to justify its privileged position in law. Here there will be two recurrent concerns. First, what role do the partisans of reason seek for reason in law and, second, is their argument equal to its task? Here we will encounter the vastly overused (and greatly underthought) argument that those who attack reason are disappointed absolutists who demand of reason way too much. Ultimately, we will see the arguments of the partisans of reason break down in unappealing displays of presumption and question begging.

Here the enchantment reaches a more profound level. The kind of enchantment experienced when reason runs out above is experienced here in the very attempt to vindicate reason—to justify its pride of place in the realm of beliefs. The stakes are greater: it is no longer this or that rational belief that is at stake, but the status of reason itself. With this raising of the stakes, the partisans of reason reveal their stake in reason. It is truth, goodness, and fate that is at stake. And with such things at stake, it is the argument for reason itself that becomes enchanted. In consequence, reason becomes the medium through which the partisans of reason believe (however erroneously) that they can secure truth, goodness, and fate. That is a fairly significant enchantment.

In the fourth chapter, "Predicaments of Reason," the argument turns to a more forthright attempt to reveal what it is about reason that leads to its transformation into its ostensible opposites: what I will call, for short, "faith, prejudice, dogma, and company." I argue that reason is a locus of predicaments. Indeed, reason may well be the sort of thing which is not possible—the sort of thing whose identity is so ideal that it can never be realized. To the extent that reason is possible, it depends on an awareness of its "predicaments," as I call them. To the extent that reason remains oblivious to these predicaments, it becomes simply a name—a venue for faith, prejudice, dogma, and company. These "predicaments" render reason precarious. But they are not so much criticisms of reason as aspects of reason itself. These constitutive aspects of reason are routinely compromised by the partisans of reason, who are almost always seeking to fortify reason by transforming it into a ruling form—"the rule of reason."

Here we encounter various kinds of enchantments that seek to bridge the gap between reason and its unthought. Here enchantment can take several different shapes. It can take the form of a single-minded attempt to erase all dogma through a continuous (though ultimately futile) critical reflexivity. Or it can take the form of an obsessive, excruciatingly elaborate (and ultimately futile) attempt to refine the frames within which and with which reason does its work. In the wake of these two kinds of excesses, it is also possible for enchantment to refuse these two avenues and to seek the sleep of neopragmatism and other forms of intellectual dormancy.

This brings us to the fifth chapter, "Divine Deceptions." There the argument is that the attempt in law to establish "the rule of reason" leads to a deification of reason. It leads, in other words, to an enchanted legal world populated with magical entities linked by magical thinking. Reason is made to posit whatever is necessary for law to seem reasoned and rational. But since law is neither reasoned nor rational (at least not throughout) it is reason that is compromised. To put it another way: Because law cannot be brought into conformity with reason, it is reason that is brought into conformity with law.

Here we get the fully enchanted world of American law. It is a world populated with the usual entities—rules, principles, rights, values, policies, and so on. But now, belief in these entities seems odd—as odd perhaps as the belief in angels, witches, and kobolds. Reason does double duty here: it assists in inducing belief in these entities and it covers for them when they fail. Reason makes the world safe for belief in these legal entities.

The enchantment does not stop here. It is not just reason that is compromised. In the sixth chapter, "The Legal Self," I argue that the self of the legal thinker and actor also takes the hit. Indeed, the incompatible demands for reason and law are reconciled in the person of the legal thinker or actor who internalizes the dissonance through a kind of cognitive impairment. The visitation of cognitive impairments on legal thinkers and actors is not a contingent occurrence, but inescapable—at least for those who, like many legal academics, want simultaneously to "think about law" and to "do it." As in many other human activities, trying to do both at once is not a felicitous combination.

1   Faith in the Power of Reason

> [A] faith that does not perpetually expose itself to the possibility of un-
> faith is not faith but merely a convenience: the believer simply makes
> up his mind to adhere to the traditional doctrine. This is neither faith
> nor questioning, but the indifference of those who can busy them-
> selves with everything. MARTIN HEIDEGGER[1]

In 1995, the dean of the Yale Law School, Anthony Kronman, was inter-
viewed on the state of his institution. The occasion for his interview must
have been pleasing: a *U.S. News and World Report* poll had just ranked the
Yale Law School first in the nation.

> It had not always been thus: At the turn of the century, The [Yale]
> Law School was for all practical purposes moribund. Its student
> body was small; its dean, Henry Wade Rogers, a recent appointee to
> the Second Circuit Court of Appeals, was a part-time teacher who
> did not want to retire, and its faculty, but for two members, were
> thoroughly undistinguished, if not better described as unknown.[2]

But this was 1995 and things were different. Commenting on the ethos of
his institution, Dean Kronman professed that what unified the Yale Law
School was "a faith in the power of reason."[3]

Now, it is well known that law school deans are tragic figures who must
routinely say outlandish things in public about the virtues of their own
institutions. Still, it is of some interest to take note that what was chosen
to praise the Yale Law School at its moment of triumph was a series of
conundrums: what unifies the law school is *faith in the power of reason.*

Far from disputing Dean Kronman's characterization, I will be arguing that he is absolutely correct—and, surely, not just about the Yale
Law School. What unifies the American law school *is,* indeed, a series of
conundrums: it is faith in the power of reason. What allows these conundrums to unify the American law school is that they are not recognized
as such. This nonrecognition, in turn, is exactly what *faith in the power of
reason* produces.

The Stakes

Faith in the power of reason is important to the integrity of American law. Indeed, the effective existence of reason can be considered a condition of possibility for what American legal thinkers and actors take to be "law" itself.

Perhaps the easiest way to understand this point is by reference to the ideal of "the rule of law"—an ideal whose core aspects are crucial to virtually all contemporary American jurisprudence. While somewhat elusive, the basic idea informing this ideal is that ours is "a government of laws not of men."[4] Implied in this formula is the notion, as the eminent (British) jurisprudential thinker Joseph Raz puts it, that the actions of people, government officials, and especially judges, will be guided by law. Among the precepts associated with the rule of law are the notions that the making of specific laws must be guided by principles that are open, stable, clear, and general. Similarly, fair procedures, notice, and impartial arbiters must be used in applying the law. Both courts and other agencies of the government must be subject to the foregoing requirements.[5]

These "rule of law" virtues require that the agencies of the state be subject to a disciplining mechanism. The disciplining mechanism is designed to constrain and control a number of human motivations (self-interest, vengeance, hate, love) and certain modes of human interaction (power, prejudice, arbitrariness, and sloth). This disciplining mechanism, so essential to the rule of law, is none other than reason. It is the possibility of a publicly accessible and recognizable reason that enables legal actors to claim that power, interest, prejudice, and personal proclivities are constrained and controlled by an overarching frame known as the rule of law.

Reason is thus an essential aspect of the rule of law. It is the mechanism by which emotions, interests, and force are supposedly kept in check. In legal analysis, any time that reason is perceived to break down, the rule of law is immediately threatened. A graphic demonstration of this point occurred during the 1980s when thinkers associated with critical legal studies ("cls") advanced the famous (or infamous) claims of indeterminacy. While there were many versions of the cls argument, the gist was that "law" as traditionally understood could not, in and of itself, yield determinate answers to legal questions. Amongst orthodox legal thinkers, these claims of indeterminacy were received with as much equanimity (and grace) as the nineteenth century greeted the death of God.

Orthodox legal thinkers treated these indeterminacy claims as an attack on the possibility of reason in law and thus on law itself. Their sense of alarm was palpable. Owen Fiss, a noted Yale Law School professor, for instance, wrote that the purpose of the indeterminacy claim

> is to deny the distinctive claim of law as a form of rationality. Law is not what it seems—objective and capable of yielding "right answers"—but rather simply politics in another guise. Judges speak the way they do because that is the convention of their profession and is needed to maintain their power, but their rhetoric is all a sham.[6]

This fear of losing reason is a fear of loss of control. This is in part why the prospect of reason running out is such a dread moment. In the understanding of legal actors, once reason is no longer in control of the decisions of an official decision-maker, arbitrariness, emotion, self-interest, politics, power, and force take over the legal machinery. From the perspective of the rule-of-law ideal, the exhaustion of reason is tantamount to an admission that legal actors do not know what they are doing—that law is, in a word, lawless.

Such a realization, when it occurs, is injurious to the professional and moral self-image of legal thinkers and actors. This point is easy to appreciate if one can imagine the legal machinery just as it is, but stripped of any pretense to being ruled by reason and the rule of law. What emerges in this picture is a legal system stripped of legitimacy. Correspondingly, what remains is an assortment of legal actors, judges, and lawyers who practice ritualized forms of violence on each other and on other people. What emerges are people engaged in incarceration, killing, plunder, extortion, and so on. As for legal academics, they are demoted to the status of thug-trainers.

On the psychological level, the loss of reason is extremely troubling. It is a kind of jurisprudential incontinence—the surrender of the professional self to all manner of uncontrollable forces. On the ethical level, loss of reason means that violence is being randomly or at least irrationally visited upon persons. Law becomes a kind of institutionally settled immorality.

For those whose very identity is wrapped up in the busyness of the legal machinery, this moment of vertigo is fraught with dread—professional dread and ontological dread. And so it should not surprise that upon reaching this moment there is an aversion of the gaze, an arresting of inquiry, a closing of the mind. Indeed, it should not surprise that at this point, the awkward moment becomes saturated with the semblance of reasoned meaning and reasoned meaningfulness. In contemporary American law, there is a whole series of soothing magic words useful for this occasion—words like

reasonable balance
reasonableness
good judgment
careful craftsmanship
pragmatism
value choice
political commitment
and so on.

These are the words one uses in a pinch to continue the legal conversation, to maintain a sense of order, to coax errant thinkers back into the fold. These are the words one uses to protect what is at stake: reason, the rule of law, law itself.

The Rule of Reason

In the rule-of-law vision, just how is it that reason keeps the various motivations, interests, and forces in check?

There is a trick here. The trick, and it is one that is performed early and often, lies in presupposing that reason is already in the driver's seat; it is already in authority. In other words, it is presumed that when reason speaks, law listens.

This is really quite a remarkable presupposition—particularly when one considers that it commands nearly universal assent, at least among legal thinkers and actors. This belief is crucial to the rule of law because it institutes reason in a privileged position in and above the law itself.

Indeed, among contemporary American legal actors, reason stands in a generally superior position to other sources of belief such as authority, experience, convention, tradition, ethics (and so on). While one does sometimes see efforts by legal actors to show that reason is grounded in our authoritative texts, in our traditions, in our experiences, most of the efforts run in the other direction. Hence, most often legal actors strive to redeem authority, experience, tradition (and so on) by demonstrating their grounding in or consonance with reason.

For contemporary American legal thinkers, the problem is not reason, but rather the other sources of belief (authority, experience, tradition, and so on). This tacit and generally unnoticed presumption is dramatically illustrated in a famous essay on authority and reason by the great British jurisprudential thinker Joseph Raz, who writes that there is a fundamental paradox between reason and authority. As Raz put it, "To be subjected to authority, it is argued, is incompatible with reason, for reason requires that one should always act on the balance of reasons of which one is aware."[7]

What is striking in this description is the asymmetry with which Raz formulates the paradox here: it is stated from the point of view of reason. The problem is not that reason may lack authority but rather that authority may lack rationality. Or as Raz puts it: Because authority requires submission even when it seems to be against reason, "submission to authority is irrational."[8] The genesis of the paradox then is that authority may not be rational, not that reason may lack authority. And indeed, Raz's resolution of the problem turns out to be little more than a demonstration that submission to authority can indeed be consistent with reason.

What matters here, however, is not the resolution offered by Raz but rather what his formulation of the problem reveals about the implicit relations of reason and authority. Evidently, for him and for his anticipated audience, it is the rationality of authority that is a problem, not the authority of reason. For him and his anticipated audience, the authority of reason is at once obvious and obviously presumed.

It is precisely through the operation of such tacit presumptions that reason is accorded a superior position relative to the other sources of belief. The presumption of American legal thinkers that reason rules is already instituted in *the unthought* of American law. It is an orientation that is already in place, even before reason is called upon to do its work.

In the unthought of American law, reason is already authorized to keep the more unruly human motivations and behaviors in check. Reason is already positioned as the source of control and as the medium of pacification.

As a source of control, reason rules from above. It rules over belief, emotions, tradition, power, politics (and so on). This is "reason as transcendence"—a reason that is distinct from and superior to the lesser more unruly legal materials and authorities. This transcendent reason is understood to enjoy a cognitive privilege over sources of belief and behavior. The more unruly sources of belief and behavior—emotion, politics, tradition, and so on—are disciplined and organized by the transcendence of reason. Reason thus has overarching jurisdiction over the content of the law itself. To the extent that there are doubts or questions about whether something is or is not law, it is reason that serves as the ultimate arbiter. Reason is the source of control.

In a second but no less characteristic image, the unthought of American law depicts reason as a medium of pacification. The materials and authorities of law are themselves already invested with the pacifying influences of reason. In this mode of "reason as immanence" the corpus of the law and its variegated materials are themselves already imbued with reason. Inconsistencies, contradictions, and paradoxes are largely suppressed. If they cannot be suppressed, then they are represented as aberrant—as unruly abnormalities in a field of law that is already largely pacified by an immanent reason. The task lies principally in bringing out this latent rationality and making it explicit.

All together then, reason is immanent in the corpus of the law (the medium of pacification) and it is also the transcendent arbiter over the corpus of the law (the source of control). Notice that this is not exactly a stable image. Reason is both in the law and above it. But let's let that slide for a few pages.

Instead, consider that in the rule-of-law ideal, it is reason that holds the whole thing together. In American law, reason is the grid of intelligibility that enables legal actors to make the connections of the law— the inferences, the deductions, the analogies, the extensions, the modifications, the limitations, the negations (and so on). It is the conceptual grid that allows legal thinkers to perform the critical operations within and upon the legal materials that mark out the legal domain. It is this grid of intelligibility that enables legal propositions and legal artifacts (rules, standards, principles, policies, values) to be linked to each other in a pleasing and intelligible network of actual and potential connections.[9] In short, it is reason that ostensibly enables law makers, appliers, and commentators to select among beliefs, to test beliefs, to monitor their modification or replacement, to map out their proper scope (and so on).

American legal thinkers and actors are more than willing to celebrate the reason of the law. Indeed, in this respect, there is a kind of "harmonic convergence" that yokes the interests of the legal academics with those of the legal practitioners.

The legal academics are quite willing to recognize the reason of law because reason is the handle that gives academics the authority to say what the law is. It is by insisting that law is the work of reason that legal academics as the custodians of reason can insist to others that their word is law.

The practitioners, meanwhile, are very much interested in representing law as reasoned, for their main rhetorical strategy in court and in other official precincts is to praise the law. To attribute reason to law allows practitioners at once to praise the law and also to extend or contract it so that the law (duly regulated by reason) comes to include their client's cause or interest. Reason is the compliment that interest pays to law in hopes of earthly reward.

In American law, not only are the other sources of belief subordinated to reason, but considerable effort is expended to make these other sources of belief more like reason itself. Legal thinkers and actors are continuously striving to rationalize these other sources of belief—to make them appear, in substance as well as in form, more like reason itself.[10]

Hence it is that sources of belief such as experience, tradition, perception, and the like are increasingly recast in the image of reason itself. They are integrated into the grid. In virtue of the relentless reworking and application of legal materials (what currently goes by the name "legal interpretation"), the various sources of belief are increasingly rationalized and thus transformed.

In part, rationalization can be counted upon to make the other sources of belief—experience, tradition, perception, and the like—more precise, more coherent, more integrated. At the same time, this precision, coherence, and integration is accomplished by abstraction and reduction. The process of rationalization transforms the manifold meanings of authority, of experience, tradition, perception, and other sources of belief into the ordered propositional aesthetic of reason. The process of rationalization—of making law rational—does not merely sort, classify, and organize; it has an aesthetic effect on *what* is sorted, classified and organized as well. Something is gained, but something is lost.

Indeed, in this rationalization process the hold of experience (as experience), tradition (as tradition), perception (as perception) is typically degraded. And it is easy to see how: to the extent that the *raison d'être* for experience, tradition, and perception becomes their conformity to reason, they lose their intrinsic power. The foreign criteria of reason such as coherence and consistency come to displace experience and perception. When rationalization has completed its work, all sources of belief must be redeemed in the court of reason.

The rationalization of American law is easily visible in the transformation of its "authoritative materials." Perhaps the most obvious and important example of this rationalization process is the perennial effort of American legal thinkers to "summarize," "restate," or "reconstruct" American law into various kinds of propositional systematizations. Hence, in the late nineteenth century, during the rise of the American law school, many legal academics devoted themselves to systematizing law into a juristic science. Then, too, there were attempts to rationalize the common law through the various codification movements. These were followed by attempts to produce uniform state laws and the various twentieth century "restatements" of the American Law Institute. In the late twentieth century, the drive for rationalization emerged in the attempt to produce something called "legal theory"—a highly abstract and systematic rendition of law as a kind of prescriptive normative discourse.

The superior position accorded to reason, together with the rationalization of other sources of belief, institutes reason as an overarching framework for the selection, testing, modification, and replacement of beliefs. It institutes a regime I call "the rule of reason." The superior position accorded to reason enables the partisans of law to assert the primacy of reason over other sources of belief (reason as transcendence). The rationalization of the other sources of belief ensures that they will be comprehensible within the categories, the idioms, and the grammar of reason (reason as immanence). It ensures that these other sources of belief can be subsumed within the rule of reason.

As suggested above, even though both modes of reason are necessary to the rule of reason, they are less than entirely compatible. In its transcendent mode, reason is cast as superior to and thus distinct from other sources of belief such as dogma, bias, prejudice, experience, perception, revelation, and tradition. This transcendent mode thus accords reason a superior position in the legal cosmology.[11] At the same time, however, the rule of reason also has an immanent mode. In this latter mode, the manifold legal materials are imbued with reason.

Central Command and the Big Tent

Not only are the two modes not entirely compatible, but the two gestures that establish the two modes of reason are themselves not entirely compatible.

Reason as transcendence is established through what might be called an "exclusionary gesture." This gesture distinguishes reason sharply from other sources or kinds of belief. The exclusionary gesture serves at once to protect the integrity of reason from contaminants and to enable the exclusion of undesirable views from law's empire. The exclusionary gesture enables legal thinkers and actors to retain a faith that the manifold legal materials and operations are organized in a coherent whole by a transcendent source: reason as *central command*.

Reason as immanence, by contrast, does its work through an "inclusionary gesture." The inclusionary gesture seeks to relax the conception of reason so as to include the other kinds of beliefs as sources or repositories of reason. The inclusionary gesture serves at once to extend the realm of reason throughout the manifold legal materials and to appropriate, coopt, and neutralize critical claims that reason depends upon other sources of belief such as emotions, belief, power, politics, and the like. Reason here is portrayed as a kind of *big tent* [12] in which all sorts of beliefs emanating from all sorts of sources are viewed as reasoned aspects of the enterprise of law.

The rule of reason includes both central command and the big tent. As central command, reason is pure, closed, formal, univocal, directive. And as the big tent, reason is practical, open, contextual, polyvocal, and dialogical. The rule of reason incorporates both of these visions. It is easy to see that a commitment to both visions will sometimes yield tension and even irresolvable conflict. Indeed, the rule of reason is a jurisprudential equivalent of having one's cake and eating it too. It doesn't work—but that does not seem to keep anyone from trying.

Hence, much of the work of American legal thinkers and actors is an attempt to express and to negotiate this tension. Interestingly, one can see this tension repeatedly expressed in various isomorphic forms throughout the constellations of American law. [13] It would be a mistake to make too much out of this isomorphic repetition. It would be wrong, for instance, to think that each of the pairs represented in table 1 are synonyms for one another, or that they entail some sort of customary alliances. Rather, the point is that each of these pairs are different ways of dividing different fields along the same kind of imagistic division. [14]

Much of the work of American legal thinkers on reason is at once the expression and the attempted resolution of this kind of tension. Much of the scholarly and judicial disagreements in American law turn upon which of the pairs is to be given primacy and how much, as well as how to specify their relations. Thus, for instance, reason as central command

Table I Central Command and the Big Tent

	Reason as Central Command	Reason as the Big Tent
"Life of the law"	"Logic"	"Experience"
Jurisprudence	Legal formalist view of law as closed, self-sufficient, self-referential	Legal realist view of law as open, socially dependent, instrumentally oriented
Institutional sources of law	Judicial review	Democratic self-government
Legal process description of sources of governmental action	Courts as the voice of reason and neutral principles	Legislatures as the fora for politics and preferences
Constitutional interpretation	Strict construction Interpretivism The written law	Loose construction Noninterpretivism The unwritten law
Utilitarianism	Rule utilitarianism	Act utilitarianism
Historical sources of law	Law	Equity
Virtues of . . .	Stable Expert Discriminating Univocal	Deliberative Dialogical Tolerant Polyvocal
Sins of . . .	Rigid Imperial Self-centered Univocal	Vague Weak Indiscriminate Polyvocal
Fairness	Fairness as uniformity	Fairness as giving persons their due
Equality	Formal or "shallow" equality	Substantive or "deep" equality
Max Weber	Formal rationality	Substantive rationality
Karl Llewellyn's styles of adjudication	"The formalist style"	"The grand style"
H. L. A. Hart's image of legal directive	"The core" of settled meaning	"The penumbra" of debatable cases
John Rawls' "reflective equilibrium"	"Principles"	"Considered convictions"
Ronald Dworkin's theory of adjudication	"The best theory . . ."	"The institutional materials"
Lon Fuller's account of dispute resolution mechanisms	Dyadic disputes (appropriate for adjudication)	Polycentric disputes (appropriate for nonadjudicatory modes of dispute resolution)
Essence of law	"The letter of . . ."	"The spirit of . . ."

can be seen as *an abstraction, a derivation, an essentialization, a representation* of reason as the big tent. But it is also possible to view the big tent as *the realization, the derivation, the unfolding, the expression* of reason as central command.

However the tension is expressed or conceptualized, it is one that does not go away. There is no way to finally opt simply for one side or the other, no way to successfully reduce one side to the other. To attempt such a resolution is to move from law to utopia. And not surprisingly, it doesn't work: every attempt to stabilize a relation between central command and the big tent collapses. Stuck with this tension, American law and legal thought remain mired in dissonance. And despite their best ambitions, legal thinkers and actors remain incapable of resolving their ambivalence toward reason as central command and reason as the big tent.

The persistence of ambivalence and dissonance is not surprising, given the intellectual pressures. Indeed, on the one side, the desire to appear intellectually *au courant* requires American legal thinkers and actors to acknowledge the social, plural, and constructed aspects of reason—its immersion in authority, experience, tradition, and vice versa. In short, they must espouse the view that in law (as in the other humanities or social sciences) reason is a big tent. At the same time, the felt need of American legal thinkers to say what the law is, to redeem law and to distinguish law from the lawlessness of prejudice, dogma, rent seeking, power politics, and so on, requires them to make a sharp distinction between reason, on the one hand, and these horribles on the other. In short, they must espouse the view that there is a reason to law and that it is in central command.

This is a tension that we will encounter in different forms throughout this book as we survey the different strategies invoked by American legal thinkers and actors to resolve the tension. Sometimes, explicit and sophisticated attempts are made to resolve the tension. Sometimes, reason simply runs out.

2 When Reason Runs Out

> This is an instance of one of the most interesting (and least commented on) moments in intellectual discourse, the moment (not at all unique to legal discourse) when the path of inquiry a practitioner is following points in a direction that fills him (or her) with horror, and as a result, the inquiry is abandoned, short of its potentially distressing conclusion. STANLEY FISH [1]

One of the most interesting and least examined moments in American law is indeed the moment when reason runs out. This is the moment when the legal argument stops. This is the moment when silence threatens to take over as it dawns on everyone that no argument could possibly be adequate to the issue at hand.

One reason this moment of impasse is seldom noticed is that it is almost never recognized as such. Instead, every effort is expended to avoid recognizing this moment for what it is. And should the moment occur anyway, great energy will be expended to end it as quickly as possible. A host of words and sounds will issue to fill the awkward silence with the appearance of meaning and meaningfulness: "Surely, the reasonable approach here is to . . . ," "Surely, we can all agree that . . . ," "Good judgment requires that . . . ," "On balance, it is clear that . . . ," (and so on). These are the sounds of legal reasoning at work: these sounds will fill the silence with a kind of jurisprudential busyness until the moment of dread is over and reason can continue on its jurisprudential way, confident, unmodified. This is a phenomenon that bears watching closely.

In one sense, one could easily think that the dread moment should occur rather frequently in American law. Indeed, inasmuch as American law often entails the clash of starkly conflicting views, the possibility that reason might run out seems real enough. Opposing parties often have radically different characterizations of the subject matter of their disputes. They not only see the same incidents differently; sometimes, they simply see different incidents.

The law reduces these incommensurabilities by forcing the opposing parties to "translate" their claims into the idioms of the law. The opposing parties must formulate their claims within the formal limits of the law itself, within the idioms of the authoritative doctrines, policies, and principles.

But just as this work of "translation" reduces the incommensurability of the claims made, it also places stress on the coherence of the law itself—forcing it to become more relaxed, more permissive, more inclusionary. Over time, the law itself comes to internalize the incommensurabilities of the claims made.

Still, American law offers a host of familiar rhetorical devices to break the standoff between conflicting or incommensurable views. Some of these devices are as simple as pointing to an authoritative legal hierarchy—for instance, the fact that one source of law (the Constitution) takes precedence over another source of law (a statute). Other simple devices involve pointing to various default settings—what are known in law as burdens of proof, presumptions, standards of review. Sometimes these devices produce a final outcome in a case—and do so in a way that seems convincing and reasonable (at least to most parties). But though these devices often seem convincing or even reasonable, the question nonetheless arises: Is it reason that is doing the work here or something else—something that might variously be called emotion, prejudice, dogma, or the like? Is reason really in control? And if so, which reason and whose reason is it that is in control?

Consider, as an example, the currently popular rhetorical device known among judges, lawyers, legal academics, and law students as "balancing." This "balancing" is what ostensibly enables the decision-maker to "weigh" competing considerations to see which shall prevail upon the others. It is balancing that enables constitutional liberties to be balanced against the interests of the state. It is balancing that enables the negligence of the defendant to be balanced against the contributory fault of the plaintiff. Indeed, at present, all manner and kinds of legal decisions are submitted to balancing tests—the conflict resolution device of first and last resort.

When balancing emerged as a significant conflict resolution device in American law in the 1950s, the hope was that it would force judges to stop hiding behind the formalisms of "wooden" doctrinal rules. The hope was that balancing would force them to articulate their reasons.[2] In the meantime, however, balancing has itself become formulaic, wooden, mechanical—in short, the repository of precisely those formalist vices that it was designed to avoid. Still, even now, the partisans of balancing and of multifactor tests continue to advertise its virtues. They say that balancing is a matter of practical reason, of judgment. It is a question of knowing which argument, which value, which reason is most important when. It is a question of making judgments and giving reasons—reasons such as:

This consideration *takes precedence.*

This principle *overrides* that one.

In this instance, certain elements *predominate.*

This value is *more directly implicated* here than that one.

(And so on.)

It is always possible to give such reasons. "Why should the First Amendment take precedence over equal protection?" "Because freedom of speech is more central to constitutional democracy than equal protection." "Why is strawberry ice cream better than vanilla ice cream?" "Because strawberry ice cream is made with fruits. Moreover, it is pink, not yellow."

It can, of course, seem outrageous to suggest that the relative standing of the First Amendment and the Equal Protection Clause is no more susceptible to reasoned analysis than a choice between vanilla ice cream and strawberry ice cream. After all, grave societal consequences turn upon the former and not the latter. And tremendous ethical, legal, and political thought has been directed at the former and not the latter. And a moral taste for equal protection does not "feel" like an aesthetic taste for vanilla ice cream. This is all true, but it only makes the point all the more vexing: the fact is that for all the ethical and political thought heaped on the constitutional question as opposed to the ice cream question, for all the doctrinal complexity that mediates legal conflicts as opposed to ice cream choices, the former is no more tractable or susceptible to rational resolution than the latter. In the end, when the castles of doctrine have crumbled, we are left talking about preferences for freedom of speech as opposed to preferences for equality. The fact that we have thought about these particular preferences a lot, and that they matter to us even more, does not suffice to transform them into something else.

Not only is it always possible to give reasons, but it is always possible to affirm that the reasons given are (really) good ones. This only pushes reason giving back another level: Why are these reasons (really) good ones? One can imagine here the unfolding of an infinite regress akin to the four-year-old's "Why, why, why?" For a while, at least, reason can easily seem equal to the task: "Because, because, because."

Indeed, one can understand the myriad doctrinal mazes of American law in exactly this way. The fields of American law are constituted by doctrine regulating doctrine regulating doctrine (and so on). So long as the legal thinkers and actors remain confined to the mazes of doctrine, they can conduct their highly specified arguments about where they are and where they should go—without ever reaching any disturbing political or intellectual questions. They are literally surrounded by mazes upon mazes of doctrine. It takes a long time to get out. It is a prolonged encounter with the why, why, whys and the because, because, becauses before one encounters the point at which reason runs out. Many legal thinkers and actors give up way before that point is reached. They check out. They are literally beaten or exhausted into (doctrinal) submission.[3]

Still, if one pursues the grounds of a balancing decision with sufficient Socratic persistence, one will again reach a point where reason seems to run out. One can acknowledge that vanilla ice cream is yellow and strawberry ice cream pink, and yet remain somewhat perplexed as to why and how that makes strawberry ice cream better than vanilla ice cream. Similarly, one can acknowledge that freedom of speech is central to constitutional democracy, yet continue to wonder why and how it is more central than equal protection.

And so if one pursues the grounds of a balancing decision with sufficient Socratic persistence, one will reach a declarative affirmation that is proffered as the authoritative and self-evident truth. Hence, it is, for instance, that the noted constitutional law professor Akhil Amar asserts that the flag-burning case of *Texas v. Johnson* was "plainly right, and even easy—indeed, as right and easy a case in modern constitutional law as any I know."[4] Hence it is that Ronald Dworkin, the preeminent American jurisprude, illustrates the powers of his ideal judge, "Hercules," by concluding summarily that "he would have rejected the principle of liberty the Supreme Court cited in the case [of *Lochner v. New York*] *as plainly inconsistent with American practice and anyway wrong.*"[5]

The Noble Scam

Ronald Dworkin, like the overwhelming majority of American legal thinkers (myself included), is not a fan of the laissez-faire decision of *Lochner v. New York.* And Akhil Amar, like the vast majority of American legal thinkers (myself included), much prefers the symbolism of the First Amendment to the symbolism of the flag.

Both preferences can easily be transposed into the more sober idioms of law and legal argument. And those who, like Dworkin and Amar, are well skilled at legal argument can be very effective in this transposition. They can effect the metamorphosis of tastes and preferences into the idioms of law in ways that seem very convincing—and not just to any audience, but to important audiences, including those at the top law schools and in the elites of the American legal profession.

All this, of course, is not nothing. And yet, it is not enough: the dread moment returns. And when it does, someone like Akhil Amar or Ronald Dworkin could very well say (and with some degree of frustration), "Look, if you don't understand why *Texas v. Johnson* is rightly decided or why *Lochner v. New York* is so wrong, well then you just don't understand the game of law." Now, legal thinkers will often say things like this, and for many of them, these kinds of arguments are very convincing.

But these arguments are a kind of scam. Now, this scam is not your run-of-the-mill scam. It is instead a "noble scam"—one with an excellent pedigree, the very best history and an affinity for the very best circles. Here is the structure of the Noble Scam: The notion is that law is a kind of game played in certain ways with certain kinds of rules and certain kinds of moves. The claim is that the game, *properly played,* will produce certain results. This is what Amar and Dworkin and countless others in effect argue. The question arises, who gets to decide whether the game has been properly played or not?

One might think that this is a difficult question, but in American law, it is not a difficult question. The answer (and it is at once clever and descriptively accurate) is that the game of law itself provides a way to determine whether the game has been played correctly or not. Of course, at this point one wants to ask, "And what way is that?" Even here we will get some answers: H. L. A. Hart, the noted jurisprudential thinker, invokes what he calls "secondary rules"—"rules empowering individuals to make authoritative determinations of the question whether on a particular occasion a primary rule has been broken."[6] Ultimately, this answer will set Hart down the path of the infinite regress and will lead him to invoke, finally, "the ultimate rule of recognition."[7] Ronald Dworkin cuts to the chase faster and simply pulls out a trump: "the very best moral philosophy."

But each time that Hart or Dworkin or some other legal thinkers go meta in this way, so can we.[8] So when they invoke "secondary rules" we ask, "*Whose* secondary rules?"—or yet again, "Secondary rules according to *whom?*" When they invoke some moral philosophy as being the best or better or sounder, we ask similarly, "According to *whom?*"

Now, American legal thinkers like Hart, Dworkin, Amar, and countless others are hardly defenseless against this move: they certainly do have an answer to the question, "According to whom?" And while their answers differ significantly in their particulars, they share at least two striking similarities. First, the crux of the answer is so institutionally well settled that it almost always goes without saying. In other words, the answer is so successful it need not actually be stated. Second, the crux of the answer is in each instance the same. The answer is "According to us"—where "us" is . . . "us" and, in the event you disagree, "definitely not you."

But still, as institutionally efficacious as the answer may be, it is not entirely satisfactory. And so, just one more time, we ask again: "But who empowered this 'us' to decide how the game is properly played?" To which the answer pops back immediately: "The game of law itself, of course." "But how do you know that?" "Well, because, we know how to play the game of law very well."

Indeed.

Notice that this is no small-time scam. On the contrary, as scams go, this one is world-class. Of course, as rendered here, the scam may seem somewhat thin. But that is because we have been focused on exposing its schematic structure. As it usually appears in "real law," the Noble Scam is rarely thin.

Moreover, it works. How does it work? First, when the authorities in the discipline of American law in fact claim to be authoritative, they are generally believed by their audience. They are thus generally successful. The scam works because of its performative dimension—the demonstrated ability of people like Professors Amar and Dworkin to be believed when they say things like "*Texas v. Johnson* is an easy case" or "*Lochner v. New York* is wrong." When people like Professors Amar and Dworkin say things like that successfully, it is because they are tapping into the authority formations that are already in place. They are saying things that their audiences already believe or already want to believe. Put Professor Ronald Dworkin in a fundamentalist church in Duluth or Professor Akhil Amar at the American Legion in Des Moines and their deployment of the scam will probably not work very well.

Now, admittedly there is an easy response to this, and that is that the fundamentalists in Duluth and the Legionnaires in Des Moines are not skilled in the practice of American law in the way that Professors

Dworkin and Amar clearly are. This may be taken as true. However, it confirms not their point, but rather mine. To the extent that Professors Dworkin and Amar are persuasive (and when they speak, legal academics listen), it is precisely because they are speaking to an audience that has already been trained to believe the kinds of things that Professors Dworkin and Amar believe. By contrast, as soon as they or their audience encounter someone (whether a citizen, a lawyer, or a legal academic) who does not agree with their legal analysis, they begin by declaring that this person has (1) made a mistake. When conversation reveals that this is not the case and that there is instead a fundamental disagreement about the identity of the game of law, they end up saying that the person is (2) "outside the game," "not playing by the rules," or, more politely, taking "the external perspective." This kind of response might be convincing if the communities of legal academics at, say, the Yale Law School (Professor Amar's home base) or NYU (one of Professor Dworkin's locales) were populated with a wide array of persons with differing political and intellectual opinions: leftists, rightists, skeptics, unbelievers, legal nihilists, and so on. In that case, we might have the sense that Professors Amar and Dworkin and their colleagues had been exposed to a wide variety of thought in a most vital way. We would have a sense that their thinking was a product of a broad and diverse exposure to thinking about law and its role in American society.

That is clearly not the case. The elite American law schools are composed almost entirely (90 percent?) of center-left democrats. They are almost all committed to a brand of scholarship that involves issuing normative prescriptions to courts, legislatures, each other, or some unknown addressee. Their jurisprudence is overwhelmingly positivist, perfectionist, doctrinal, and court-centered. Almost all of them understand their scholarly mission to be the improvement of law through the construction of ingenious interpretations of the authoritative legal judicial or legislative materials.

The point, then, is that when legal thinkers get together in their professional fora and nod agreeably with each other that *Texas v. Johnson* was right, there is nothing surprising about the consensus. On the contrary, what else could one expect? Christians believe that Jesus is the son of God; Communists believe that The Party is the vanguard of the proletariat; and American legal academics believe that *Lochner* was wrong and *Texas v. Johnson* was right. Given the kinds of subjects included and excluded within each of these three communities, what else could one possibly expect?

Nodding Heads Agree

The point here is that the circularity of the Noble Scam is not just conceptual: the circularity has a social dimension. It extends beyond the speaker through the audience's beliefs, hopes, desires, aspirations, and preexisting commitments. The Noble Scam works, not because it is conceptually circular but rather because *the beliefs of the audience are themselves part of the circle that forms the argument.* And this explains as well why the audience does not experience the circularity of the Noble Scam as circular. For that audience, the circle is not a circle at all, but quite simply the way things are.

If one thinks about it, not only is there something circular about the Noble Scam, but there is also something about it that seems faintly un-American. Just what kind of game is it where some of the players not only play the game, but get to referee and to "reconstruct" the rules as they go along? This sounds awfully much like being a judge in one's own case.[9]

It is in the midst of such statements that the dread moment returns. Once again reason runs out. This is the moment at which reason leaves off—leaving the beliefs upon which it (reason) rests and upon which it (reason) does its work unthought.

Later, we will ask about reason's relations to this unthought. For now, what is to be noticed is that a great number of thinkers (both in and out of law) are quite content to leave this unthought undisturbed—indeed, to a large extent, unnoticed.

How is the unthought eclipsed from view? We have just seen how. For one thing, those called upon to decide a case will often confuse or conflate what they take to be self-evident and authoritative with the work of reason itself. The result is that a great number of varied and incompatible beliefs are passed off as if they were the products of reason. If reason never seems to run out, it is precisely because at the point where it seems that it would run out, one always finds something to be self-evidently true. One finds, for instance, that justice trumps efficiency (or vice versa). One finds that fidelity to precedent is more compelling than policy arguments (or vice versa). It is with such judgments that the self-evidently true—the unquestioned—is routinely passed off as the work of reason itself.

A striking example of this phenomenon—striking because of its esteemed provenance—is the philosopher John Rawls's pronouncements on what "public reason" requires in the context of abortion. Rawls posits that the main values implicated are due respect for human life, the ordered reproduction of political society, and the political equality of women.

Upon consideration of these values, he draws his conclusions: *"[A]ny reasonable balance* of these three values will give a woman a duly qualified right to decide whether or not to end her pregnancy during the first trimester." The reason this is so, according to Rawls, is that "at this early stage of pregnancy, the political value of the equality of women is *overriding."* [10] Now, particularly if one agrees with Rawls (as I do), this can seem like a reasoned argument: "Yes, the political value of equality is overriding." But then a moment's thought: "Just what makes it overriding, apart from saying it is?" It is precisely in this idiom of reason ("reasonable balance," "overriding," etc.) that what the author takes to be self-evidently true is represented as the ineluctable product of reason itself.

And it is precisely because these beliefs *are* held to be self-evidently true that it becomes so easy for the already persuaded to presume that these beliefs are themselves the work of reason. Nor is this just a matter of strategic self-presentation. On the contrary, it is often a sincere gesture among American legal thinkers and actors to parlay beliefs that are familiar, comfortable, widely held, long-standing, and pleasing (in short, self-evident) into the work of reason itself.

Again one wants to ask, how does this occur? How is it that unexamined beliefs are parlayed into the work of reason itself?

Reason Rules

One of the things that legal thinkers and legal actors are trained to believe is that in law, reason is already in power. In law, reason is already authoritative. Indeed, this is likely why it does not occur to legal thinkers to question the authority of reason. The question does not arise, for the answer is already presumed: Reason already rules.

In some respect, the belief that a discipline already empowers its members to think rationally is one shared by all disciplines. The analytical philosopher, the political scientist, the psychologist arrive on the scene of inquiry already understanding themselves to be possessed of knowledge, methods, techniques, procedures, and protocols. They already understand themselves authorized to apply their disciplinary reason to their field.

In this respect American law exhibits a striking difference. Not only does the American legal thinker understand himself or herself authorized to apply reason to the field, but (and this is the striking difference) he or she presumes that the field (the cases, the statutes, and so on) are themselves already organized in the image of reason. In other words, the typical American legal thinker arrives upon the field of law—the materials, as it were—presuming that this field is already largely a reflection of reason. (Reason as a big tent.) What is more, he or she typically presumes that this field, the materials, are themselves already responsive to reason and reasoned argument. (Reason as central command.)

This is the conventional assumption—and while it is possible to find some American legal thinkers who do not share this view—the overwhelming majority of legal thinkers do. For lawyers and judges, it is necessary to indulge this assumption regardless of whether it is true or not. Legal argument proceeds on the assumption that the law is rational and, if not, that it can be made more so. For lawyers and judges, there is almost never any percentage in starting with the view that the corpus of the law is not rational.

American legal academics also take the authority of reason for granted. It is presumed that law is already accessible and even responsive to rational deliberation. Law is already cast in reason's image, and the legal thinker is already in possession of a reason that can analyze and explain this law. Notice that the confidence of the legal thinker in reason here is not restricted to a belief that he or she will be able to sort out rationally what these judges, legislators, and lawyers are doing. The hubris goes considerably farther. The confidence of the legal thinker is that he or she will be able to show the rationality of what these actors are doing usually on their own terms and at the very least, in ways consistent with their own terms.

Now, this view is taken for granted by virtually all American legal thinkers—even though it is, once one thinks about it, a controversial (if not improbable) presumption. Why, after all, would one presume that the interested actions of state agents (known as judges) attempting to resolve difficult disputes in circumstances of serious information deprivation and strategic behavior would be ruled by reason or rationality? Why in particular would one presume that such adjudication would exhibit rationality when indeed the laws that inform this adjudication are often the product of rent seeking, power politics, outright deceit, and other questionable strategic behaviors?

3 The Arguments for Reason

Reason is what we say it is. ANONYMOUS

The superior position accorded to reason, together with the rationalization of other sources of belief, institutes reason as an overarching framework for the selection, testing, modification, and replacement of beliefs. In short, it institutes "the rule of reason." The superior position accorded to reason enables the legal thinkers and actors to assert the primacy of reason over other sources of belief. The rationalization of the other source of belief ensures that they will be comprehensible within the categories, the idioms, and the grammar of reason.

In sum, for the great many who practice American law or American legal thought, reason rules. For them the appeal of reason is so strong that they take it that a reasoned case for reason has already been made (and won). But how was it won?

After all, in law, reason confronts significant competition as a source of belief. There are authority, tradition, custom, convention, force, power, experience, emotion, faith, dogma, and so on. These too are sources of belief. How did they come to be subordinated to reason? Similarly, in law, reason confronts hostile worlds—worlds hostile to the very possibility of reason itself. These are the worlds of radical pluralism, of radical incommensurability, worlds of paradoxes and undecidabilities, worlds resistant to identity thinking. How is it that reason has vanquished its competitors and established its rightful rule?

These questions gain a special poignancy when one considers that reason's triumph could not have been achieved by just any means. It was not an option for reason to triumph by invoking faith, prejudice, dogma, and company in its cause. On the contrary, as its champions insist, what distinguishes reason from these other sources of belief is its deliberative self-questioning character. Reason, it is said, requires consideration of the arguments made against it. It requires attention to its own possible biases and distortions.[1] So, the question returns: Just how is it that reason vanquished its competition and established its rightful rule?

This is a question that will occupy our attention over several chapters. For now, we will address the questions in narrow terms, by considering the kinds of arguments that have been made by American legal thinkers on behalf of reason.

The Reasonableness of Reason

Perhaps the most common argument on behalf of reason is a claim that the use of reason is itself reasoned. Reason is portrayed as a rightful or truthful way of gaining knowledge or understanding of the world. This is a contestable claim, for, a priori, there is no particular reason to believe that the world sought to be ruled by law is consonant or compatible with reason. A priori, there is no reason to believe that the social or the psychological is organized along rational lines. It may, of course, be necessary for reason itself, as Kant argues, to make such presuppositions.[2] But to acknowledge that point does not establish the reach of reason. One must consider the frustrating possibility that the psychological and the social may well be organized in ways discordant from reason. This is a possibility that matters to reason itself. Indeed, reason must always be concerned about its own adequacy relative to its field of application.

Sometimes, the partisans of reason attempt to dispose of such concerns with general "philosophical" arguments aimed at justifying the reasonableness of reason. These arguments are aimed at vindicating reason even in worlds whose very characters resist the aesthetics of reason. As an example of such an argument, consider a recent attempt by Professor Cass Sunstein to reconcile reason and incommensurability. In a long article on this topic, Professor Sunstein strives to show that various goods (eating apple pie or reading Wittgenstein) are sometimes incommensurable, in the sense that their value is not reducible to a single metric such as the utilitarian's "util" or the microeconomist's "dollar." Sunstein aims to celebrate this irreducibility.

But not too much: as a self-announced partisan of "reason," he deems it crucial to show that incommensurability does not preclude making choices "on the basis of reasons." It is crucial, in other words, to show that while certain aspects of our world may be characterized by incommensurability, nonetheless reason remains an effective overarching frame that enables reasoned choice. It may be difficult to choose between Wittgenstein and dessert, but one can, as he puts it, "give reasons."

As we join Professor Sunstein, he has already developed much of his argument about incommensurability in the law. He is now about to encounter a disturbing possibility—what he calls the problem of "radical incommensurability." This is the problem posed when, indeed, the various goods or valuations are so divergent that choices cannot be evaluated in terms of reasons. Or as Sunstein puts it: "On this view, choices among incommensurable options are impossible on rational grounds, or relevant goods are so radically incommensurate that there is no process by which human beings can reasonably choose among them. Reasons run out."[3] Now this is the point where things become interesting. Reason gains its appeal precisely because it promises to enable what Sunstein calls reasonable choice—in other words, the kind of choice that is informed by the evaluation of competing reasons. All of this, of course, presupposes that all competing considerations can fit within a single frame comprehensible to the one doing the evaluation and the choosing. In short, it presupposes a *monistic aesthetic.*

Radical incommensurability presents a challenge to this sort of monistic aesthetic precisely because it holds that the world is irreducibly plural in character. It presupposes that the world is organized in various regions or sectors or modes of cognition or kinds of discourse that are radically different and that do not all fit within a single frame. Things become interesting because, faced with radical incommensurability, reason is now confronted with a serious challenge.

Here one could expect intellectual inquiry to take any number of turns (some more plausible than others). Indeed, the possibilities here are numerous.[4] For American law, this is largely unexplored territory.[5] But what happens? Rather than savor the encounter of reason with incommensurability as an interesting intellectual problem, rather than use this confrontation to inquire into the limits of reason, Professor Sunstein shuts down. Indeed, in an eighty-two-page article on the topic of incommensurability and reason, the encounter of the two in their vital, mutually antagonistic form is reduced to a mere two paragraphs. Sunstein writes:

> I think that it is very rare for this form of incommensurability to occur in the intrapersonal case. People often face incommensurability—either in the sense that I have emphasized or in the Raz-Anderson sense—without being at all paralyzed about what to do, and while thinking, *rightly,* that their judgments are based on reasons.[6]

This, it turns out, is the sum and substance of Professor Sunstein's answer to the problem of radical incommensurability: an assertion, a rhetorical trick. The answer is an assertion that the problem of radical incommensurability is "very rare." And what is the evidence for this empirical judgment? Sunstein says: People who face incommensurability often think "*rightly* that their judgments are based on reasons."

This is the kind of reasoning that puts one in mind of the exemplary logic no doubt used by the church during the Inquisition: "Do witches exist? Of course, witches exist. Why, we burn them all the time."[7] Professor Sunstein's confusion (like that of the inquisitors) lies in conflating a belief about something with the thing itself. It is, in short, a pre-Kantian kind of confusion.

Indeed, simply because people say or even feel that they use reason to make a choice is hardly evidence that they do. As a general matter, people will often say many wonderful things about their own thought processes and how these operate. Indeed, they can be counted upon to say that their beliefs are the products not merely of reason, but of wisdom and a good heart, and so on. Generally, however, such first-party reports are not terribly reliable sources of information as to the actual identity or functioning of those thought processes. Simply because it is pleasing to believe that one's own beliefs are reasoned hardly makes them so.

We might take Professor Sunstein's argument as a case in point. As a partisan of "reason," and "reason giving," he is committed to practicing what he preaches. He is, in short, committed, as he puts it, to "giving reasons." But in the end, when reason is challenged, the only thing he offers are assertions.

What Sunstein does is treat his own (and his audience's beliefs) as if they were the ineluctable product of reason itself. This is the rhetorical strategy he uses when he writes that people who face incommensurability often think "*rightly* that their judgments are based on reasons." Here the fact that people *believe* that their judgments are based on reason is used to conclude that their judgments *are in fact* based on reason. But, of course, all this depends upon whether people in fact *rightly* believe this. The term "*rightly*" has to do a lot of work here, and yet there is nothing to support it besides Sunstein's own conviction in the truth of his own assertions.

Why would Sunstein's argument be persuasive? Again, if his argument is persuasive at all, it is only because his reader is already prepared to believe the conclusion. Indeed, the emptiness of Sunstein's argument becomes apparent when one substitutes "divine revelation" for reason. Hence, consider this revision: "People often face incommensurability without being paralyzed about what to do and while thinking *rightly* that their judgments are based on divine revelation." If one does not already believe in "divine revelation" does the assertion announced in the word *"rightly"* help the argument?

No.

Now, one might think that the banal weaknesses of Professor Sunstein's arguments are traceable to his advocacy. But this is not clearly so. The kind of rhetorical trick that Sunstein deploys to salvage "reason" is very old and very common. Paul Feyerabend, for instance, detected the same rhetorical trick among the classical Greek philosophers who sought to submit the pluralism, the incommensurability, the abundance, the polycentric character of Greek myth and tradition to the rule of the overarching monism of reason:

> Almost all of them praised oneness (or, to use a better word, monotony) and denounced abundance. Xenophanes rejected the gods of tradition and introduced a single faceless god-monster. Heraclitus heaped scorn on *polymathi'e,* the rich and complex information that had been assembled by commonsense artisans and his own philosophical predecessors, and insisted that 'what is wise is One' . . . . Parmenides argued against change and qualitative difference and postulated a stable and indivisible block of Being as the foundation of all existence. Empedocles replaced traditional information about the nature of diseases by a short, useless, but universal definition. Thucydides criticized Herodotus' stylistic pluralism and insisted on a uniform causal account. Plato opposed the political pluralism of democracy, rejected the view of the tragedians such as Sophocles that (ethical) conflicts might be unresolvable by 'rational' means, criticized astronomers who tried to explore the heavens in an empirical way and suggested tying all subjects to a single theoretical basis.[8]

This subjugation of the many to the one, of pluralism to monism, of polytony to monotony, of difference to sameness, and so on, is an essential precondition to the rule of reason. If the world—like the world of the Homeric gods—is not subject to a unitary conceptual matrix, then reason cannot perform its most basic operations: its equivalencies, its negations, its analogies, its transitive moves. In short, it cannot rule.

For reason to rule, it must necessarily presuppose a world that is consonant with its own monistic aesthetic. Reason must presuppose that the world can be apprehended in its own aesthetic, its own categories, its own operations. This is the process of rationalization that we saw at work with authority, experience, and tradition. There are two aspects that are particularly important here: *identity* and *frame*.

Identity first. If reason is to do its work then the things it must work with must be the sorts of things upon which reason can operate. Poetic meaning, coercive pressure, habitual response, in their authentic forms, are not the sorts of things that are accessible to reason. It is only when these things have been transformed into a stable propositional form—into "concepts" or "ideas"—that reason can be brought to bear upon them. If reason is to access and rule over other sources of belief, then they must be cast in a form—in an aesthetic—that conforms to the aesthetic of reason. They must be reducible to stabilized identities that can take the form of p and q—as opposed to sometimes p and sometimes not p, undecidably p, or yet again p tending toward not p (and so on). If reason is to rule here, it must have beliefs with which it can work, beliefs cast in its own ordered propositional image.

Frame second. Not only must the identities of the things upon which reason works be accessible to reason, but these things must be located within a frame within which reason can rule. There must be a continuous web—wherein reason can perform its crucial operations, its equations, negations, and orchestration of other relations. To rule, reason must presuppose a world that is subject to a unitary frame where everything that might be relevant to a "reasoned choice" can be adequately represented, conceptualized, and considered.[9] Gaps, paradoxes, aporia, discontinuities, disjunctions, undecidabilities, ambiguities, ambivalences (and so on) are obstacles that preclude reason from performing its crucial operations. They are, in short, precisely the sorts of things that must be liquidated, reconfigured, or subsumed if reason is to rule.

To put it another way, the rule of reason depends upon the possibility of fitting all the considerations within a single frame. In this limited sense, the rule of reason presupposes a monistic aesthetic—that is, an aesthetic in which all that might be relevant to choice can be adequately represented, conceptualized, and considered. It does not matter whether this monistic aesthetic is presumed to exist in the world as such (objectivism) or in our modes of understanding and apprehension (subjectivism) or in our language. What does matter is that, one way or the other, the world be rendered amenable to this monistic aesthetic.

In a radically incommensurable world, however, this monistic aesthetic is explicitly denied. Faced with a world of the many, of the plural, of the incommensurable, of difference, of nonidentity (and so on), reason has nothing *to do* except recognize its limitations. For the partisans of reason, such a prospect is quite frustrating. These are people who not only seek to praise reason, but to do things with reason—to expand its dominion. And it is understandable that they should attempt to vanquish these reason-defying worlds through means other than reason. To a significant degree, this is precisely what has happened. As Feyerabend suggests, the strategy of the classical Greek philosophers who sought to submit the unruliness of the many to the monistic rule of reason was itself not reasoned, but rhetorical: tricks and insults.[10]

More than a couple of millennia later, the situation remains, in this respect, largely the same. In the late twentieth century, what is the answer of the partisans of reason to pluralism, to radical incommensurability, to radical pluralism, to difference, to nonidentity (and so on)? Assertion. Bluff. Assertion and bluff—or as Sunstein puts it: "Most of the time, however, radical incommensurability is not present. Both people and societies *do make* choices among incommensurable goods, *and they do* so on the basis of reasons." Apparently, that's just the way it is.

For those who refuse to submit to this monistic rule of reason, Sunstein tells them that they are "wrong." They are wrong, it turns out, precisely *because* they refuse to submit to the monistic rule of reason. Or again, as Sunstein puts it: "[I]t is possible that one participant in the discussion is wrong even if, or *because, he is not subject to persuasion; he may reject reason-giving altogether* or be unable to see good reasons even when they are invoked."[11]

That is not an argument. This is a combination of authoritarian posturing and shallow circularity—a thin version of the Noble Scam. What we have here is an imperial assertion that reason rules. This assertion is then followed by the claim that those who do not accept this truth are wrong. But why would anyone not already persuaded accept such a claim—or find it even mildly convincing?

The short answer is that they wouldn't. The argument for reason here is not a reasoned one. On the contrary, the argument for reason here depends precisely upon short-circuiting any thoughtful consideration of the grounds of reason. And this short-circuit is characteristic of the closed circle of conversation of American legal thought. The partisans of reason rarely engage with their opponents. And when they do, often enough it is to engage in smug dismissals (Sunstein) or, as we shall see below, in gross mischaracterizations (Nussbaum).

This is not an accident: the imperial dismissive tendency and the tendency to mischaracterize, as will be seen, has important links to reason itself. As will be seen, it is the imperial ambition to use reason to rule that leads to smug dismissals. And it is the monistic aesthetic of reason that leads it to an impoverished and abstracted mode of understanding—one whose internal coherence is achieved at the expense of a misprision of all that is not reason. Ironically, and not without a certain poetic justice, these tendencies of reason to attempt to vanquish its opposition turn out to be self-destructive of reason as well. Pursued long and hard enough, these tendencies can lead to the metamorphosis of reason into its traditional enemies: reason cast as faith, prejudice, dogma, and company. These are all points to which we shall return.

In Praise of Reason (The Argument from Virtue)

The partisans of reason often recommend reason by virtue of its commendable associations. Hence, they often depict acceptance of reason as morally admirable, while depicting its rejection as morally wrong. This sort of argument, with its eminent theological pedigree, resonates deeply throughout Western culture.

In fact, the argument that reason is allied with the good is but a special instance of a more general rhetoric—notably, a providential alliance between reason and all the notable virtues. In this providential congruence, all the notable virtues just happen to be allied on one side (the side of reason) in a great struggle against all of the vices on the other side. Hence, reason is depicted as good, divine, true, beautiful, powerful, and healthy. Meanwhile, the rejection of reason is cast as profane, false, evil, ugly, weak, and diseased.[12]

The elegant symmetry of this rhetorical economy yields undeniable advantages for its proponents. The elegant convergence of all the notable virtues on one side (the side of reason) conveniently reprieves mortals from ever having to sacrifice one virtue for the sake of the others. Meanwhile, the convergence of all the notable vices (over on the other side) conveniently enables the thoroughgoing demonization of the opposition, removing any possibility that it might have any redeeming virtues.

It is important not to overstate the point: this simple rhetorical economy is not invariant in American (legal) culture. But it does recur with sufficient regularity that it is important to take note of its operations. One of its most prevalent manifestations is in the ideal of "the rule of law." In support of the rule of law, it is said that the partisan of reason commits himself to certain established procedures of argument and proof that are publicly accessible. By virtue of his commitment to these procedures, he is also committed to following them even when these procedures require actions against his own interest, whim, and arbitrary desire.[13] In this way, the partisan of reason is said to exemplify the ethical life. In American law, the argument is given perhaps its most articulate voice in Herbert Wechsler's famous article on neutral principles and in Lon Fuller's work on the rule of law.[14] In turn, these arguments draw much of their rhetorical force from the golden rule and Kant's categorical imperative.

In contrast to the partisans of reason, it is said that the critic of reason can make no commitment to leading the ethical life. It is said that those who question or reject reason deny the rule of any overarching, publicly accessible procedures of argument and proof. Hence, unable or unwilling to recognize such procedures, they can make no ethical demands upon themselves. They are, in short, without ethics. It is even said that this is the state of affairs they seek to bring about—that at heart, they are really unsocialized hedonistic scoundrels who seek only to advance their own self-interest and to free themselves of guilt.[15]

But again this claim is not so much an example of reason in action as it is a series of questionable rhetorical tricks. Two tricks are of particular interest here.

The first trick lies in equating the scoundrel who rejects the rule of reason with all who might reject the rule of reason. Now, it is true that scoundrels will refuse to honor such established procedures when it suits their interests. (Socrates' Piraeus is not merely a port, but also a state of mind.) Still, it does not follow that because the scoundrel will not abide by the rule of reason, all who reject the rule of reason are scoundrels motivated by selfish interest and a desire to be free from ethical disturbance. To draw such a conclusion would be a rather banal logical error.

And yet it is made often enough. As an example, consider Martha Nussbaum's recent attacks on the work of Jacques Derrida. Martha Nussbaum is not merely a preeminent philosopher but also a noted classics scholar. And so, on her way to do battle with Derrida, she recounts the story of the skeptical philosopher Pyrrho. It seems Pyrrho was on the deck of a ship during a storm. Pyrrho witnessed the passengers anxiously trying to protect themselves, their possessions, and their loved ones. Meanwhile, a pig, also on the deck of the ship, was contentedly eating at its trough. Pyrrho pointed to the pig and said, "The wise person should live in just such freedom from disturbance."[16] Nussbaum interprets the

passengers' anxieties and actions as resting on sound normative commitments. As for Pyrrho, she understands him to be counseling the suspen-
sion of normative commitments. Less subtly, she understands him to be
advocating the contented life of the self-gratifying pig.

In a series of none-too-subtle rhetorical transformations, Nussbaum
will depict the critics of reason as advising us to live the life of the pig. Indeed, in Nussbaum's arguments, Derrida will be equated to Pyrrho and,
ultimately, to the pig. Nussbaum asks why critics of reason like Derrida
set up their "skeptical" arguments as they do. She answers:

> [T]here is no convincing answer to this question that does not men-
> tion something like the skeptic's freedom from disturbance as an
> organizing goal. Why does Derrida, interpreting Nietzsche, reject
> the difficult task of trying to decide what is the best reading of the
> complicated text? . . . Derrida turns away from the task of deciding
> what to praise and what to commend, and toward an interpretive
> strategy that leaves him free to play and cleverly indulge himself.
> Can we explain this, in the end, without mentioning his preference
> for the condition of free play itself? [17]

In short, for Nussbaum, Derrida is a self-indulgent person who seeks
freedom from the rule of reason so that he can read texts to mean whatever he wants them to mean, bound by nothing, obliged to no one. He
is, in Nussbaum's view, just like Pyrrho's pig.

This conclusion rests on a very poor reading of Derrida's discussion of
the free play of the text and its relation to subjectivity. It is an interpretation that erroneously presumes that because there is free play in the text,
somehow it is the individual interpreter who is *in control* of this free play
and who thus "*chooses*" what meaning the text must have. This understanding is explicitly considered and rejected by Derrida. Derrida's free
play is the free play of the text, not the free play of the individual subject.
And the individual subject is no more capable of escaping the free play
of the text than anything else.[18] It is only because Nussbaum projects the
categories of Anglo-Saxon American moral philosophy into Derrida's
text, most specifically the liberal individual subject and his rationalism,
that she comes up with such an impoverished moralizing reading of
his work.[19]

So much for Nussbaum's reading of Derrida. We could quibble about
her lack of "charity" to the "other"—namely, Pyrrho and the pig. (Equanimity, after all, is not an unqualified human evil, just as normative com-

mitment is hardly an unqualified human good.) But Derrida, Pyrrho, and the pig are not the focus of concern. Instead, what is of concern is the character of Professor Nussbaum's argument.

The crucial point is that once again, we are faced with the pretense of a reasoned argument when none is presented. What Nussbaum does is present a rhetorically *plausible* motivation for denying the rule of reason—that of the pig, that of the scoundrel, namely self-indulgence—as if it were *the only possible* and *the actual* motivation for Derrida's views. But, she furnishes no demonstration of either point—neither that it is the only, nor that it is the actual motivation. And, there cannot be any such demonstration absent a consideration of what she does not even pause to consider, namely, that one might seek to reveal the free play of the text for any number of motivations—to edify, to educate, to warn, to obstruct, to dismantle (and so on).

Nussbaum's rhetoric is quite familiar. It is an instantiation of a more generalized practice in which the questioning of reason, its identity, and its jurisdiction is variously identified with self-indulgence, self-centeredness, abnormality, deviance, lack of self-control, personality defects, mental illness, and generally immoral or unethical behavior. Typically, this unflattering characterization of the critics of reason is accompanied by a glowing self-congratulation of the partisans of reason. Those who remain committed to reason are praised for their selflessness, altruism, self-mastery, personal soundness, courage, and admirably moral behavior.

Again Professor Nussbaum's rhetoric is exemplary in this regard. Her essays are full of moral praise for her readers who are depicted as (really) good people—people who care deeply about the fate of the poor, the oppressed, and so on. And in this depiction, there is again no excess of subtlety. Thus, in an essay in the *Harvard Law Review,* Nussbaum invites the reader to identify with a young woman, Nikidion, who will face some profound ethical dilemmas. The reader is invited to identify with this young woman, who is obviously also an alter ego for Nussbaum herself. Nikidion not only has "a very intense interest in intellectual success and security," but she is also a wonderfully moral person. She is, in Nussbaum's own words, deeply committed

> to a definite view of human flourishing and good human functioning. . . . Because she has concluded that the good of other human beings is an end worth pursuing in its own right, apart from its effect on her own pleasure and happiness, she is committed to thinking hard about the political and economic conditions in which other

people live, and to doing whatever is in her power to promote people's capabilities to function well. Through these commitments she interprets herself and the world. . . . She notices keenly the impediments to good human functioning that her society has placed in her path: the absence of political rights for women, for example, and women's perilous economic condition. She feels anger at her present state and fears for her future. At the same time, she notices the situation of others, and, because she is a social being who considers the flourishing of others to be an important goal, she responds to their perceived misery with compassion and urgency. In this way, by thinking about human needs and about the good, she multiplies her sources of disturbance. Poverty, slavery, ill health, the deaths of children—in all these misfortunes of others she finds additional burdens for herself.[20]

This praise of Nikidion's intellectual prowess and ethical wonderfulness goes on at length—in bouts of ever more intense displays of author-reader self-congratulation. No doubt, for those readers always prepared to believe the best about themselves, this rhetoric works well. Certainly, in the world of American legal thought, this kind of moralistic posturing has had its share of rhetorical success. Indeed, before "Nikidion" (a.k.a. Martha Nussbaum) there was "Hercules" (a.k.a. Ronald Dworkin).

As common as it is, there is nonetheless something discernibly tendentious about this kind of moral posturing. For one thing, it is truly striking that the advocacy of utterly conventional, if not banal, values in the *Harvard Law Review* can be portrayed as if it were itself a moment of real moral triumph. Somehow the *advocacy* of goodness, rightness, justice, courage (and all those other values that are routinely castigated by audiences everywhere) is presented as if it were itself a courageous act—at once good and just.

This is the point where the rhetoric of the partisans of reason goes too far. There is nothing particularly courageous in arguing for what people already want to believe: that justice is real, that reason rules and so on. The advocacy of such pleasing views is something to be expected not only from the ethical person, but from the scoundrel, the careerist, the opportunist, the self-indulgent, the lazy, the slothful, and so on. Consider this: If you were a scoundrel and you wanted to advance your social (or academic) station, would it not behoove you to *say all sorts of nice things to power?* Would you not represent the law of the powerful as the very unfolding of reason on earth, their politics as the instantiation of ethics in action, their beliefs as knowledge itself? In short, is not the ethical praise of reason (when reason is whatever we are already doing) precisely the sort of thing to be expected from a latter-day sophist?

By contrast, if one were an ethical person, not a scoundrel at all, would one not, upon witnessing all this ethical praising of power, begin to question not only the uses of reason and ethical discourse, but their actual role, their actual identity, their actual character? Indeed, in such circumstances, one might well begin to wonder if the relentless celebration of the rule of reason was not a way of avoiding more difficult ethical problems—a way of pretending that social and political life is already ruled by reason, that the uses of power are already responsive to ethics (and so on)? Similarly, one might come to believe that this presumption that reason rules is a way of shielding oneself from ethical disturbance and ethical strife.

Notice that now the ethical valences have been reversed. Now it is the scoundrel who seeks refuge in the soothing matrices of reason to avoid ethical disturbance. It is the scoundrel who wants ethics reduced to the aesthetic of a train schedule. And correspondingly, now it is the ethical person who is driven to question the identity and the character of reason and reasoned ethics.

It is important not to make too much out of this. Specifically, the point here *is most definitely not* that the partisans of reason are all scoundrels, *nor* that the critics of reason are all ethically wonderful. Rather, the reversal of valences here is designed to show that there is no necessary ethical or conceptual alliance between reason on one side and goodness, rightness, justice on the other. Those who can be counted upon to invoke the dominant ethical discourse of their society include both scoundrels and ethical persons. Similarly, there is no necessary ethical or conceptual alliance between the questioning of reason, on the one hand, and immorality, personality defects, or mental illness, on the other. Those who can be counted upon to question the dominant ethical discourse of their society include both scoundrels and ethical persons. In order to discern who is a scoundrel and who is an ethical person, we would need something more specific in the way of argument—something more specific that certainly has not been forthcoming from the partisans of reason.

The upshot is that the claim that reason is somehow in alliance with ethical behavior remains an assertion—more a case of ethical bullying than reasoned argument. And this is so because the claim rests upon the circular presupposition of the conclusion sought. The ethical superiority of reason to other sources of belief—experience, custom, tradition, insight, intuition, revelation, disclosure, (and so on)—is only plausible if the world is already cast in the *monistic* aesthetic of reason. In that case, reason and reason giving will have some purchase on that world. The partisans of reason will be speaking the language, the categories, the grammar in which that world is already organized. But if the world is organized in terms of the many, the plural, the incommensurable, the different, then reason is not speaking the language of that world. And if it attempts to rule nonetheless, reason becomes a violence. As Paul Feyerabend put it:

> But if the world is an aggregate of relatively independent regions, then any assumption of universal laws is *false* and a demand for universal norms *tyrannical:* only brute force (or seductive deception) can then bend the different moralities so that they fit the prescriptions of a single ethical system. . . . [F]rom the very beginning the salesmen of a universal truth cheated people into admissions instead of clearly arguing for their philosophy. . . . They praised argument— *they* constantly violated its principles.[21]

The Argument from Fate

There is yet a third kind of argument that is often made on behalf of reason. It is the argument from fate—reason's equivalent to Pascal's wager. In Pascal's wager, the conclusion is that it is better to wager on God's existence than on his nonexistence. If God exists, it would be truly disastrous to deny his existence. On the other hand, if he does not exist, very little is lost in believing in his existence.

The argument in Pascal's wager is based on the affirmation of a cost asymmetry. Indeed, the argument is ultimately addressed to self-interest and does its work by tallying up the costs and benefits.[22] While the argument is often described as a display of reasoned argument in favor of belief in God, in the last analysis it has less to do with reason than with self-interest. In a passage subsequent to the famous wager, Pascal's imaginary interlocutor invites Pascal to give up on reason altogether and simply follow his own self-interest:

> Endeavour, then, to convince yourself, not by increase of proofs of God, but by the abatement of your passions. You would like to attain faith and do not know the way; you would like to cure yourself of unbelief and ask the remedy for it. Learn of those who have been bound like you, and who now stake all their possessions. These are people who know the way which you would follow, and who are

cured of an ill of which you would be cured. Follow the way which they began; by acting as if they believed, taking the holy water, having masses said, etc. Even this will naturally make you believe and deaden your acuteness. . . .

Now, what harm will befall you in taking this side? You will be faithful, honest, humble, grateful, generous, a sincere friend, truthful. Certainly you will not have those poisonous pleasures, glory, and luxury; but will you not have others? I will tell you that you will thereby gain in this life, and that, at each step you take on this road, you will see so great certainty of gain, so much nothingness in what you risk, that you will at last recognise that you have wagered for something certain and infinite, for which you have given nothing.[23]

What is interesting about this passage is that it reveals that the engine for belief here is not so much reason as interest. One believes in God because it is in one's interest. And it is a measure of how little reason is involved that ultimately Pascal's interlocutor counsels the abandonment of reason altogether. As the philosopher Slavoj Žižek succinctly puts it, the ultimate advice is to leave reason behind, mimic ideological ritual—in short, "act *as if* you already believe, and the belief will come by itself."[24]

In American law, we have the same sort of argument. Only in law, God is replaced by reason. In law, the argument for reason begins by addressing the reader's reason. But then slippage sets in and ultimately the appeal is to the reader's interest. In terms of formal structure, we have almost perfect reenactments of Pascal's wager.

Hence, the argument is often made in American law that one should believe in reason because the alternative is to surrender to chaos or power or some other distinctly unpleasant state of affairs.[25] Bruce Ackerman, a leading liberal thinker, recently upped the emotional ante by personalizing the gesture. Ackerman wrote: "Are you quite sure that it is in your self-interest to scoff at the very idea of citizenship, when *you may later want to protect your own hide* by appealing to others to take a broad view of the public good?"[26]

Sometimes legal thinkers even try to squeeze some ontological mileage out of such arguments—implying that because we very much need reason, therefore it must exist or at least be available on the menu of our metaphysical options. Here is a wonderful example of the deployment of Pascal's wager in favor of reason drawn from the work of Professor Suzanna Sherry. In this work, Professor Sherry is confronting certain "epistemological pluralist" views that deny the plausibility of reason. In a wonderfully circular gesture, she rejects these views, because, . . . well, because they deny the plausibility of reason: "What then, is wrong with epistemological pluralism? Its primary failing is that it leaves no way to resolve disputes between epistemologies except by recourse to power. If we cannot reason together, then all we can do is arbitrarily select winners and losers. The winners will necessarily be those with power."[27] The assumption here is that reason must be available to resolve disputes because the default alternative (namely, power) is just not acceptable. This is part of the creed of American legal thinkers. What we see here is the strikingly odd, yet pervasive belief that human life and human law must always already be responsive to normative desires for reason, order, progress, and the like.

Often, in American law, the Pascalian argument for reason is less explicit. The argument is expressed in a widely assumed view that in law things have to come out all right: Justice, goodness, and even progress have to be possible; law has to be capable of coherence; our thoughts must be capable of consistency; our selves must be autonomous and integrated. In other words, various idealized states are taken as given—as states of affairs that are not only possible (and attainable) but to which we are in some sense entitled. The rhetorical structure of the Pascalian move is extremely simple. It goes like this:

> If we want to believe in X (where X is something really desirable like "Heaven" or "reason" or "order" "or "progress" or "the rule of law" or "transformative change"), then Y must exist.

> Ergo Y exists. (Or in a pinch: Ergo, it is "as if" Y exists.)

This kind of argument is ubiquitous in American law. Joseph Beale, one of the great late-nineteenth-century formalists, used this kind of argument to refute the claim that the common law can only change if the courts change it. Beale's solution—every bit as clever as any piece of medieval scholasticism—was that the common law was itself always already changing.

How did Beale know this? Because in order to believe that the common law is progressive (i.e., in order to believe X) it is necessary to believe it is already changing (i.e., we must believe Y). Ergo: The common law is already changing. In Beale's words:

> It is certain that the common law changes; not merely the common law of a particular jurisdiction, but the common-law system in gen-

eral. This must be true, or the science of law, differing from all other sciences, would be unprogressive. The law of today must, of course, be better that that of seven centuries ago, more in accordance with the general principles of justice, more in accordance with the needs of the present age, more humane, more flexible, and more complex.[28]

This kind of argument is used to bolster belief in all manner of what I call "desirable X's"—God, reason, progress, whatever.

To give an example from American law, consider Professor Philip Soper's description of the influential jurisprudence of Ronald Dworkin. Professor Soper opines that Dworkin's approach to law—trying to make the legal materials "the best they can be"—is familiar in analytical philosophy. Soper writes:

> The approach Dworkin has adopted is a rather ordinary and familiar one within modern analytic philosophy. It might be called the "coherence" or "consistency" approach. . . . [I]t resembles description. Unlike description, however, it does not stop with simply recognizing the various possible meanings for terms like legal obligation. Instead, it proceeds to identify one particular point of view that stands in special need of clarification—clarification in the philosopher's sense of showing *what must be assumed if we are to be consistent in the concepts we employ.*[29]

This assumption that it is somehow useful to go about rendering our concepts "consistent" or "coherent" is an approach that underwrites a great deal of analytical philosophy as well as American law. Why we are entitled to concepts that are "consistent" or "coherent" and why social practices must partake of such attributes are questions that are rarely asked or answered. Perhaps the answer is that "coherence" and "consistency" are necessary aspects of what we call "law." But that answer just kicks the inquiry back another level: To what extent is that kind of "law" possible? That, too, is a question that is rarely asked.

A great deal of legal reasoning simply assumes such desirable states as plausible, so long as one commits to reason and reasoned deliberation. Given the plausibility of such normatively desired states, the rejection or abandonment of reason is seen as wasteful and unnecessary. The plausibility of achieving those normatively desired states is what secures both the possibility and the desirability of belief in reason, just as in Pascal's wager the plausibility of achieving the recognition of a grateful God is what secures the possibility and the desirability of belief in God. In neither case is there any argument offered that God or the normatively desired states are real in any deep sense. There is only the assumption (in both cases) that it would be nice if they were real, accompanied by an argument that little is lost in pretending they are real (if they are not) while a great deal is lost in pretending that they are not real (if they are).

Sometimes the Pascalian argument for reason is cast in more apocalyptic terms. It is said that either we must choose reason or chaos. Reason is said to be a prerequisite for being able to think, to carry on understanding, to continue intelligent legal conversation, to fashion workable law. At its most extreme, the commitment to reason is cast as a prerequisite for a happy ending to human history.

At other times, the argument is cast in consequential form: Only through commitment to reason will all the other good things follow. The problem with this argument is that consequentialism is played out on the turf of history. And absent a showing that history is already subject to reason, such prognostications about the consequences seem somewhat speculative.

At still other times, the argument is cast in a quasi-transcendental form—very much reminiscent of the method of analysis presumed by the analytical philosophers. It is said that by engaging in argument, in dialogue, one is perforce already practicing reason itself. Any dialogical argument that attempts to refute this point becomes, as Jürgen Habermas puts it, "a performative contradiction."[30] It becomes, in short, the doing of precisely that which one claimed to be impossible. *But that is true only if the initial condition is met—namely, that argument and dialogue presuppose a commitment to reason.*[31] And that, putting circularities aside, necessarily remains undemonstrated within the performative contradiction argument. Once again, it is the desirability of believing that our communications are consonant with reason that serves to bolster our confidence that it is. But, as nice as this may be to believe (God was once quite a comfort too), the point remains undemonstrated.

The question-begging aspect of Pascal's wager and its contemporary equivalents go even further than this. If one thinks about it, Pascal's wager and its contemporary equivalents are exercises in preaching to the choir. Pascal's wager does not take seriously the possible value of a world without God.[32] Indeed, if Pascal's wager is able to trivialize the costs of believing in a God that doesn't exist, it is only because it devalues the possibility of a world without God. In that sort of world—valueless as it is presumed to be—the cost of simulating faith is small. The instrumental costs of prayer and Sunday worship are trivial. And if there is no God, then there is no morality, no motivation for avoiding inauthenticity or bad faith. If that world is indeed valueless, then the costs of feigning piety and faith are negligible. But if there is value to a world without God (as a Nietszche might claim) then the cost of bad faith is not simply the cost of participating in meaningless rituals. It is nothing short of foregoing the value of the world.

The short of it is that the cost asymmetry that the microeconomists might detect in Pascal's wager only emerges as a stark cost asymmetry from the perspective of those who already believe in God—those who, in other words, are prepared to trivialize the value of a world without God. For the rest of us, Pascal's wager seems far less like a sure bet. The same is true when we are talking about reason. Faith in reason is not without its opportunity costs—namely, the costs involved in sacrificing the other sources of belief, sources such as experience, custom, convention, intuition, disclosure, perception, awareness, understanding, and so on. This is a point to which we will turn toward the end of this book.

Reason's Raison d'Être

Now it might be said that the argument here has been unfair to reason. It might be said that the argument has been too demanding of reason—that the demands for a reason uncontaminated by belief are simply too stringent, that they are impossible to meet. This is a characteristic objection made against the critics of reason.[33] It is said that the critics of reason present an image of reason that is too narrow, too strict, and therefore unattainable. The objection is that the argument is unfair in insisting upon a distinction between reason and belief.

Before addressing this matter, we should pause to consider from where this demand for such a distinction issues. This demand that reason be distinguishable from belief (in a strong *either/or* sense) is one that issues precisely from those who have faith in reason themselves. It is *they* who are so insistent upon maintaining a superior status for reason to what they take to be the other sources of belief—experience, custom, tradition, insight, intuition, revelation, disclosure, and so on. It is they who insist that reason is entitled to a preferred place in our intellectual, political, and legal life.

But if reason is entitled to rule in this way (and for them it is) it can only be because reason is at once distinct from and superior to the other kinds of belief systems. In turn, however, this normative wish for reason to rule depends upon reason actually having a certain ontological identity—one that gives it a status distinct from and superior to mere belief. It is only if reason is distinct from and superior to other forms of belief that reason is entitled to such an exalted status. If, by contrast, it should turn out that reason is just another kind of belief or is indistinguishable from belief, then reason would no longer be entitled to such an exalted status. In terms of its entitlement to rule, reason would lose its "raison d'être." More than that, reason would have nothing left to do but dethrone itself and relinquish its exalted status.[34]

This is why the demands here are not unfair to reason. The stringent demands that reason be distinguished from other forms of belief do not issue from the critics of reason—but rather from the desire of those who have faith in reason, those who wish to maintain its rule.

And it is readily understandable why they should insist on such stringent demands: should reason become indistinguishable from belief, it would relinquish any claims to an ontological identity that would authorize its superior normative status. Once reason is demoted to the status of belief—belief like other beliefs—it loses its claim to rule. This is why those who have faith in reason are and must remain so demanding of reason itself; must in fact insist that reason distinguish itself as superior to other forms of belief. And it is why, ultimately, those who have faith in reason resist the dilution of "reason" in the swamp of belief.

They are not prepared, they remain quite unwilling, to relinquish the various privileges that they accord to reason. They refuse to allow reason to take its place among dogma, bias, prejudice, experience, custom, perception, revelation, and tradition as just another source of belief. And the reason is simple. There is a great deal at stake: for the partisans of reason, it is reason itself that serves as the overarching organization of the world they inhabit. For them, reason is *the web of intelligibility*. And *that* is not something to be given up lightly.

4 Predicaments of Reason

> We have found, indeed, that although we had contemplated building a tower which should reach to the heavens, the supply of materials suffices only for a dwelling-house, just sufficiently commodious for our business on the level of experience, and just sufficiently high enough to allow of our overlooking it. The bold undertaking we had designed is thus bound to fail through lack of material—not to mention the babel of tongues, which inevitably gives rise to disputes among the workers in regard to the plan to be followed. IMMANUEL KANT[1]

To rehearse any more examples of the failures of the partisans of reason would become tedious. We can see now that there is an argument that the partisans of reason should be making that is, nonetheless, not being made. This argument, the one not being made, is a reasoned defense of reason. Instead of making such an argument, the partisans of reason resort to dogmatic assertions, to rhetorical bluster, to political posturing, to ethical bullying, and to shallow circularities.

Why?

Why would intellectuals—thinkers at the forefront of their fields—engage in such practices? And why, of all persons, would those who claim a commitment to reason engage in such practices?

There are a number of answers. One answer is actually the occasion for some empathy with the partisans of reason. The answer is this: The request that they defend reason on the basis of reason is at once impossible and yet mandatory. As the philosopher John Searle recently put it:

> There are a number of such general frameworks where the demand to justify the framework from within the framework is always senseless and yet somehow seems incumbent upon us. Thus, although one can prove that a particular argument is valid or rational within the criteria of rationality and validity, one cannot prove within those criteria that rationality is rational or that validity is valid.[2]

There is a paradoxical structure that haunts the attempt to ground reason in reason. The parties who attempt such a justification or grounding must always already rely on that which they are attempting to justify or ground.[3] They are thus threatened by the possibility of a shallow circularity—perhaps even a circularity that is at odds with the idea of reason itself. If, by contrast, the attempt to justify or ground reason is accomplished in ways different from reason, then the effort will have missed the mark. It will have failed to ground reason in reason—resting reason either on dogmatic assertions or on the empty chasm of an infinite regress. All together, this vexing array of disappointing possibilities is called the "Munchausen trilemma": the attempt to ground reason must in the end rest on (1) infinite regression, (2) circularity, or (3) dogmatic assertion— none of which, of course, can satisfy the grounding ambition.[4]

This inability to justify reason on reason's grounds may help explain the curiously unreasoned character of the arguments made by the partisans of reason: the arguments from reasonableness, virtue, and fate. It helps explain the resort to dogmatic assertions, to rhetorical bluster, to political posturing, to ethical bullying, to shallow circularities, and to ad hominem arguments.

It may be, of course, that the tendentious rhetoric of the partisans of reason is ultimately a betrayal of reason. ("With friends like these . . .") Indeed, this sort of rhetoric might be understood as a pathology of reason—an attempt to deify reason, to fortify reason by transforming it into a seemingly more stable kind of belief—something on the order of faith. This is a point to which we will soon turn.

But not yet. For now, however, the question is: Where does reason lead us concerning its own status? It leads us to precisely the point at which we have now arrived. Reason leads us to a recognition of its own limitations—and to a recognition of its own immersion in belief. It leads us to recognize that reason depends upon belief.[5]

And this is so in several ways.

Belief in, for, and through Reason

First, of course, it is necessary to have belief in reason—for reason itself is not self-grounding. Reason does not rest on its bottom. There must thus be a belief that reason serves some desired virtue such as goodness, rightness, truth, or beauty. One believes in reason because reason is right or true (Sunstein), because it is good (Nussbaum), or because it is in one's interest (Pascal's wager).

This brings us to a second sense in which reason is dependent upon belief. Not only must there be belief in reason for reason to do its work, but there must be beliefs upon which reason can do its work. Without beliefs, reason has nothing to work on. But what are those beliefs that reason can work on and are they themselves rational? This is an important and difficult question. It is difficult because it is extremely easy to engage in extraordinarily intense processes of reasoning with beliefs that are themselves not rational. One need only advert here to the meticulous ratiocination of the medieval scholastics or the nineteenth-century phrenologists.[6] As such examples show, it is quite possible to apply rational procedures in a very systematic, purposeful, conscientious, and yet ultimately irrational way.

For the contemporary American legal thinker or actor, it clearly *feels* as if a belief in principles or doctrines is very different from a belief in angels or a belief in nineteenth-century bump science. It feels more reasonable, more certain, more obviously true.

But, there's the rub: feeling that some belief is reasonable, certain, or obviously true is not a sign of its rationality. Instead, it is a sign that the belief is indeed one that is believed—very much so. It may be, of course, that the strong degree of conviction evidenced in the believing of the belief has something to do with the belief's rationality. But then again, it may well not. Indeed, those for whom strong beliefs come easy—those for whom things are self-evidently and obviously true—can hardly claim an unblemished track record in the annals of rationality.

To put it bluntly, the problem is this: To those who are caught within the grips of belief (which is to say, everyone) the contents of their irrational beliefs do not produce warnings of their irrationality. On the contrary, to those who are caught within the grips of beliefs, those beliefs are self-evidently true. In fact, to those who believe, those beliefs seem so self-evidently true that it would be irrational to disbelieve them.[7] And yet, as so much of the history of intellectual endeavor reminds: Garbage in/garbage out.

There is yet a third way in which reason is dependent upon belief. Reason is itself a kind of belief. Indeed, whether we are talking about the principle of noncontradiction, or the idea that like cases should be treated alike, we are talking about beliefs. Now it may be that reason is a special kind of belief. It may be that reason, in at least some of its guises, is peculiarly methodical. It may be as well that reason is a kind of second-order belief—a kind of belief about belief. And it may be as well that reason aspires to be a kind of transcontextual belief—the kind of belief that is thought to hold good across a wide variety of different contexts. One would expect all these characterizations to be advanced if, indeed, the role of reason lies in *selecting, monitoring, and replacing other beliefs*. The point, however, is that regardless of these possibilities, reason nonetheless remains a kind of belief.[8]

The upshot of all this is that reason is brigaded by belief. Reason is motivated and sustained by belief. Reason works on beliefs. And reason is itself a form of belief. All of this raises the question once again. If reason is entitled to rule, what precisely distinguishes it favorably from other forms of belief? The answer to this question is hardly clear.

Critical Reflexivity and Frame Construction

One thing, however, is clear: Reason cannot be indifferent to this predicament. Reason cannot take its dependence upon belief with indifference. The cost of doing so—the cost of blithely presuming the rightfulness or the efficacy of reason—is that reason becomes transformed into its traditional enemies: faith, dogma, prejudice, and company. And as we have seen, such a metamorphosis is all too easily achieved. All that is required is the unthinking equation of one's own beliefs with reason itself.[9]

Reason thus imposes certain requirements on its deployment. Some of these are commonplace. Hence, reason itself requires an examination of the processes by which information and claims are made, expressed, and recalled. Reason demands an examination of the bases and the grounds for reasons given. It demands as well correction for biases. Reason requires as well a certain degree of engagement—a consideration not just of the reasons for something, but of the reasons against it as well.[10] All of these self-critical turns are themselves implicit in the very notion of reason. As Kant put it:

> Reason must in all its undertakings subject itself to criticism; should it limit freedom of criticism by any prohibitions, it must harm itself, drawing upon itself a damaging suspicion. Nothing is so important through its usefulness, nothing so sacred, that it may not be exempted from this searching examination. . . . For reason has not dictatorial authority; its verdict is always simply the agreement of free citizens, of whom each one must be permitted to express, without let or hindrance, his objections or even his veto.[11]

A survey of the intellectual history of reason would reveal that many champions of reason have insisted upon the need for reason to question its dominion, its roles, its uses, its identity, and the like. There has been, in short, an insistence that reason itself is *critically reflexive*.[12] Enlightenment thinkers such as Kant, for instance, were particularly concerned with the proper scope and limits of reason.[13] The masters of suspicion, Freud and Marx, used reason in the effort to reveal its psychological or ideological distortions. More radically still, Derrida questioned the very scene, the very language within which the reasoning of philosophy purports to happen. All of these thinkers have insisted upon different kinds of critical reflexivity—different not just in their orientation and direction, but also in terms of their sweep and their radicality.

Critical reflexivity can be helpful insofar as it foregrounds the character of the problems presented—their provenance, scope, relevance, tilt, meaning, and so on. By revealing "the context of genesis," the contexts within which the problem arises, critical reflexivity may help provide a more useful formulation of the problem, a more helpful understanding of one's relation to the problem (and so on).

But sometimes a single-minded fascination with the contexts of genesis simply eclipses the original problem in favor of an inquiry into the context of genesis. Critical reflexivity can easily become its own end. A ceaseless critical reflexivity thus has but one objective: to peel away the successive layers of context, of genesis, to follow the trail of the infinite regress wherever it may lead.

Where does such critical reflexivity lead? If left unrestricted, it leads to ever more radical examinations of the frames and orientations within which reason operates—frames and orientations established in language, culture, institutions, practices, the self, and so on. Critical reflexivity unsettles the given contexts. By turning attention on the frames and orientations (the contexts) within which problems are posed, issues are raised, solutions are recommended, critical reflexivity unsettles those contexts.

But ironically there is one context that is left unexamined, undisturbed —that is the context of critical reflexivity itself. Ironically, this most antiformalist, frame-destabilizing activity succeeds in establishing its own formalization. Indeed, ceaseless critical reflexivity transforms all potential objectives for the use of reason into one objective—namely, an interminable inquiry into how reason and reasons are generated and constituted.

Left unrestrained, critical reflexivity can thus become pathological. And this is so in two ways.

Distraction. In one sense critical reflexivity can distract attention from the original object of inquiry to something else such that the initial problem, the initial inquiry, is never resolved. Left unrestrained, ceaseless critical reflexivity reorients reason away from any given objective—solving a problem, formulating a solution[14]—to a single objective, namely, the pursuit of an inquiry into the genesis of one's reasoning and reasons. In some cases, this reorientation will be a good thing—because the initial problem, the initial inquiry was not interesting, or not tractable. In some cases, however, this reorientation will be a bad thing; it will succeed in distracting attention away from pursuing an interesting or important initial inquiry. Deciding which is which is, of course, not something that critical reflexivity can tell you.

The Return of Freeze-Framing. The second thing wrong with ceaseless critical reflexivity is that it transforms itself into its own worst nightmare. Critical reflexivity is often motivated by antiformalism, by a desire to dismantle and move beyond the grids in place. And, of course, insofar as critical reflexivity unsettles contexts, it seems to have a powerful antiformalist bent. And it does. But it also has its own formalizing tendencies. Indeed, ceaseless critical reflexivity ultimately enshrines itself as the ruling formalism. There is an ironic sense in which critical reflexivity transforms all contexts into a single context: the search for the contexts of genesis. Every thought becomes a step backward on the trail of the infinite regress. Everything else is eclipsed.

We need to encounter one more irony. Critical reflexivity is often viewed as a destructive activity. Yet, if we are right about the single-mindedness of critical reflexivity, it is not just destructive. On the contrary, in transforming all contexts into an occasion for an inquiry into the context of genesis, there is a sense in which critical reflexivity is really quite constructive. It is constructive of—what else?—its own frame of inquiry. Indeed, the persistent questioning of how thoughts, ideas, values, are formed secretes its own frames of analysis. Critical reflexivity constructs rational frames that may be employed to examine the rationality of various ideas or actions. In a phrase, critical reflexivity is also a kind of *rational frame construction.*

This, of course, may seem odd since we are accustomed to thinking of critical activity as "destructive," whereas we tend to think of the creation of frames as "constructive." But this may turn out to be an overly simple view of the matter. An illustration from American law may help here. Consider this passage taken from Professor Henry Hart's famous (or infamous) article, "The Time Chart of the Justices." He asks a series of questions:

What exactly was the scope of the holding in . . . [x]? What exactly was the scope of the holding in . . . [y]? Did not one or both of them carry the principle upon which it rested to an undue extreme? In any event, can the two principles be fitted together? Is the principle of . . . as it was applied in . . . consistent with the policy of . . . applied as it was in. . . ? [15]

Notice that these questions—typical of American legal analysis—can be understood both as rational frame construction and as critical reflexivity. They are a kind of critical reflexivity reduced to the frame of law. And they are the rational frame of law turned upon itself in critical reflexivity.

This conjunction is not an oddity—neither in law nor elsewhere. On the contrary, we will find, if we look, that rational frames are a kind of formalized critical reflexivity and that critical reflexivity is often the institution of a rational frame.

There are a number of things that are quite important about this recognition. First, whether something is identified as critical reflexivity or rational frame construction is a matter of perspective. Inasmuch as critical reflexivity institutes its own rational frames, and inasmuch as rational frame construction has its own critically reflexive character, it is hardly clear which is which.

Second, whether some activity is to be criticized for the excesses of critical reflexivity or excesses of rational frame construction is not obvious. Suppose we find Professor Hart's questions above truly obsessive, truly obnoxious in their intensity. Are we to criticize these questions because they exemplify an excess of critical destructiveness? Or because they exemplify an excess of rationalist formalization? Both?

Third, there are important lessons for those who see themselves as champions of critical reflexivity as well as for those who see themselves as proponents of rational frame construction. For those who are committed to critical thought: Critical reflexivity is *not* invariably or even intrinsically liberating or emancipatory. On the contrary, pushed to its limits, it is single-minded and formalistic. For those who are committed to the construction of rational frames: There is nothing intrinsically constructive about instituting rational frames. On the contrary—and here American law is an obvious example—constructing rational frames is also destructive: it supplants and destroys everything else. As one example, consider that nothing destroyed the common law quite so well as the advent of the "constructive" contributions of consequentialist reasoning, policy analysis, and, ultimately, law and economics.

All of this, of course, leaves reason in quite a predicament. Critical reflexivity cannot be trusted. Can one, then, place one's faith in rational frame construction? In a sense, we have already seen that the answer is no, for rational frame construction is also critical reflexivity. And, indeed, it can be seen that rational frame construction, even when it does not seem overly critical, can nonetheless suffer from precisely the same pathologies as critical reflexivity.

Indeed, by constantly striving to perfect and rationalize its frames, reason produces ever more refined, ever more intricate, ever more specialized frames. Pushed too far, rational frame construction will, like critical reflexivity, liquidate its contexts—both the contexts from which it originates and the contexts within which it operates. In either case, this liquidation proceeds in the same way as in critical reflexivity: Rational frame construction substitutes for these contexts its own frames. It becomes, in a word, an *alienated* form of thought (and life). Rational frame construction loses interest in the contexts and becomes focused on the elaboration of its own dynamic, its own structure. This is, of course, precisely the accusation that antiformalists make against those they cast as formalists. It is the claim that the legal realists of the 1920s and 1930s leveled against the Langdellians; it is the claim that the critical legal studies thinkers of the 1980s leveled against the legal process liberals.

It turns out, then, that there is less tension between critical reflexivity and rational frame construction than first seemed. That is because both critical reflexivity and rational frame construction share the same two moments. Both critical reflexivity and rational frame construction share a context-constructing moment and a context-dissolving moment.

What distinguishes the two is that rational frame construction prides itself on what it constructs. Critical reflexivity on the other hand, prides itself on what it destroys. In both cases, this self-representation is partial, is less than wholly accurate. Another way to put the matter is that rational frame construction wants only to see what it constructs (not what it destroys). Critical reflexivity, by contrast, wants to see only what it destroys, not what it creates.

Both critical reflexivity and rational frame construction can thus be said to be idealized self-representations of their own activities. They both focus on only one part of their activities. Once this point is understood, the predicament can be restated. There is very much a tension between the context-destroying and the context-creating aspects of reason. What is in question is how much, when, to what extent should reason strive to construct contexts or to destroy them.

This is not a question that reason can answer. One might think that destruction is inherently bad and construction inherently good, but this view, while pervasive, is woefully inadequate. Indeed, it all depends upon what is being destroyed and what is being constructed. And it does not take too much effort to recognize that whenever something is being destroyed, something is being constructed (and vice versa). The important question in each case is, what? There is nothing unqualifiedly good about nurturing or supporting evil, or anything unqualifiedly wrong with destroying waste. In short, it seems wrong to base one's ethical or political commitments on one's attitudes to verb forms without examining the identity of the direct object. In the end, we are without baselines—and embarrassed by way too many contexts—to try to adjudicate this kind of question.

One thing is clear. The unrestrained deployment of critical reflexivity and rational frame construction evolve into pathological forms. It is important to understand that this doesn't say much of anything. Not saying much of anything at this juncture is precisely my point: we are without grounds, reason cannot tell us the appropriate mix. And it is a big mistake to suppose that this is the sort of question that reason can answer. To suppose that reason can answer this sort of question is precisely to fall sway to the enchantment of reason.

But the enchantment of reason is precisely what happens in law and legal thought. Reason must be pressed into service to resolve these difficulties. The desire to resolve the tension can lead to any number of proposed solutions. One can try, borrowing from Rawls, to deploy some version of reflective equilibrium. Viewed in this way, the appropriate mix of critical reflexivity and rational frame construction is a matter of bringing our assessments of both in accordance with our considered intuitions. One could try for a Kantian solution—one that is echoed in the jurisprudence of Ronald Dworkin. Hence, one could allow reason to strive for what Kant calls "the greatest unity," given the materials furnished by our experiences. One can invoke a pragmatic solution and suggest that the question is one of context.

These are all plausible answers. Perhaps they will even yield in any given context what are called "good" results. And yet despite their plausibility, there is something fundamentally wrong with all these answers. And it is this: *They are all in their own way invitations to go to sleep. They are all invitations to forget the predicaments of reason.* Each of these answers is little more than a pleasing name attached to the predicaments of reason—

the unsteady relations of reason and belief. And the question of what is the appropriate mix of critical reflexivity and rational frame construction is again a question of belief.

Reason may, of course, be turned upon these beliefs to help ascertain whether they are reasoned or not—and whether they can be counted upon to serve virtues such as truth, goodness, utility. But reason can only do so much to evaluate the content of these beliefs. It can only do so much because once again such an evaluation will itself be grounded and shaped on unreasoned beliefs—in short, on an unthought.

This is a point that has been recognized in different ways by many of the continental critics of reason: Nietzsche, Gadamer, Foucault, Derrida, Lyotard, Deleuze (and so on). They have all insisted (albeit each in his own way) that reason is fatally indebted to belief (or more broadly to something other than reason itself).

Nietzsche writes:

> Every great philosophy so far has been . . . the personal confession of its author and a kind of involuntary and unconscious memoir.[16]

Gadamer writes:

> We are always within the situation, and to throw light on it is a task that is never entirely completed. This is true also of the hermeneutic situation, i.e. the situation in which we find ourselves with regard to the tradition that we are trying to understand. The illumination of this situation—effective-historical reflection—can never be completely achieved, but this is not due to a lack in the reflection, but lies in the essence of the historical being which is ours.[17]

Foucault writes:

> Expressing their thoughts in words of which they are not the masters, enclosing them in verbal forms whose historical dimensions they are unaware of, men believe that their speech is their servant and do not realize that they are submitting themselves to its demands. The grammatical arrangements of a language are the a priori of what can be expressed in it.[18]

Derrida writes:

> [O]ne cannot do anything, least of all speak, without determining (in a manner that is not only theoretical, but practical and performa-

tive) a context. Such experience is always political because it implies, insofar as it involves determination, a certain type of non-"natural" relationship to others. . . . Once this generality and this a priori structure have been recognized, the question can be raised, not whether a politics is implied (it always is), but which politics is implied in such a practice of contextualization. This you can then go on to analyze, but you cannot suspect it, much less denounce it except on the basis of another contextual determination every bit as political.[19]

Lyotard writes:

Nothing can be said about reality that does not presuppose it.[20]

Deleuze and Guattari write:

A concept always has the truth that falls to it as a function of the conditions of its creation. Is there one plane that is better than all the others, or problems that dominate all others? Nothing at all can be said on this point. Planes must be constructed and problems posed, just as concepts must be created.[21]

While all these critics have very different twists on their descriptions of the unthought (and its implications) nonetheless they all converge in denying the autonomy of reason. They all attempt to reacquaint reason with its dependence on the unthought.

It is, of course, possible to try to reveal the identity of the unthought. But there is always a catch. And, in one sense, the catch is always the same. Every attempt to reveal the unthought always already occurs from within a particular situation, orientation, perspective, enterprise, project (and so on) that prefigures, that anticipates the identity of the unthought. There is no unmediated access to the unthought. The unthought will always already be apprehended from within the matrices, the grammar, the orientation of a particular thinking (grounded in its own unthought).

This is why the names, identities, and other dimensions of the unthought vary from thinker to thinker: "will to power" (Nietzsche), "forms of life" (Wittgenstein), "the unconscious" (Freud), "the hermeneutic circle" (Gadamer), "the project" (Sartre), "power/knowledge" (Foucault), "interpretive communities" (Fish), "différance" (Derrida), "habitus" (Bourdieu), "the Background" (Searle), "the plane" (Deleuze and Guattari), and so on. This retreat of the unthought from the thinking that would reveal it also helps explain why these various formulations of the unthought remain elliptical and vaguely mystical. At the same time, it is also true, that depending upon which of these formulations of the unthought is operative, the unthought becomes either more or less perspicuous, more or less tractable, more or less retrievable, more or less catastrophic.

Gadamer's hermeneutic circle, for instance, presents a version of the unthought that is eminently perspicuous, tractable, retrievable. Gadamer institutes a cheerful ontology—one that enables an incremental convergence of the meanings of interpreter and interpreted. Derrida's "différance," by contrast, can barely be articulated (without negating its meaning) and introduces a permanent noncoincidence of meaning with itself. In each of the cases, the possibility (or impossibility) of retrieving and articulating the unthought has been anticipated in the very conceptualization of the unthought and in the thinker's own relation to the unthought. It is this anticipation, this naming of the unthought—whether "différance" or "hermeneutic circle" or whatever—that remains, in each case, unthought, indeed, perhaps even unthinkable.

And the problem is that regardless of whether one adopts a "comfortable" or an "apocalyptic" orientation, there remains a chasm, a rift, a discrepancy between the thought and the unthought. The very taking up of language as a mode of expression already anticipates the character of the unthought—its identity and configuration. And there is no getting around, behind, or beyond this chasm, rift, discrepancy.

Working at a Useless Task

The truly vexing thing is that this gap between the thought and the unthought can never be bridged—neither through critical reflexivity nor through rational frame construction. Thus not only are the projects of critical reflexivity and rational frame construction in uneasy (and indeterminable) opposition, but each is in important (not all) senses doomed to fail. And, what is more, they will fail for the same reasons.

While critical reflexivity unsettles contexts, it also institutes and establishes other contexts. There is, in the end, no way to take a final inventory of the contexts within which one is operating. And this is so, as Stanley Fish demonstrates over and over again, in several ways at once.[22]

Displacement. Every attempt to articulate the context within which one is writing or speaking establishes a new context. It creates a displacement that brings about a new relation between the author, his thought, and the audience. For instance, consider the typical gesture among contemporary American academics to emphasize their ethnic, gender, and sexual identities. To say, as some academic authors say, "I am speaking here as a Harvard-educated white male," brings about a change in the relations of the author, his thinking, and the audience. Once the author identifies himself as a "Harvard-educated white male," the context within which he thinks has now changed to one where both he and his audience understand that his particular ethnic and social identity may have some ostensible bearing on what he thinks. He is an author conscious of the fact these particular features may affect his worldview; a new context has thus been constructed for his thought—namely, the context of being aware of his ethnic and social identity. (And so on . . . in a *mise en* abîme.) Of course, it is often the case that some of these changes of context have only trivial implications. But sometimes the implications will not be trivial at all. The trick would be in knowing which is which.

But the same thing is true of rational frame construction. No sooner does reason create frames, categories, and operations within which to understand or manipulate its object than it establishes a kind of displacement between this object and its framing of that object. As soon as reason frames an object, gives it a name and accords it a location within reason's frame, reason is no longer unambiguously referring to its object. It has instead always already displaced that object by giving it a name—one whose properties or characteristics are no longer purely a function of the object itself, but also a function of reason's frame.

There is thus an ironic sense in which reason as rational frame construction, while striving to talk about the "external world" is talking about itself—its own character and constitution. This displacement is unavoidable. As soon as reason names its object, that name selects and abstracts from the object itself and does so from within the necessarily limited and necessarily partial perspective of reason. The object which was thus the initial focal point of interest for reason thus becomes displaced by the name that reason has given it. In performing its necessary operations, reason as rational frame construction is thus constantly displacing the objects it seeks to name, talk about, and manipulate in favor of its own names, frames, and operations. The specter of disciplinary solipsism and disciplinary self-referentiality thus haunts rational frame construction as much as it haunts critical reflexivity.

Ironically, this necessary and unavoidable displacement by reason of its object is rarely visible to those who engage in rational frame construction (and who generally decry critical reflexivity). It is worth pondering why. Those who pursue rational frame construction are generally not so naive as to think that the frames that reason constructs are identical to the reality. On the contrary, they understand that there is some sort of discrepancy between the description and the reality, between the frame and its objects, between the theory and its referents. Indeed, they will often characterize their descriptions, frames, and theories as "a first approximation," "an ideal type," "a model," "a paradigm," and so on. In such usages, the distance between description and reality, frame and object, theory and referent *seems* to be acknowledged. They will nonetheless defend their constructions on the grounds that these are useful to enable identification and evaluation of the real: of reality, of real objects, of real referents. But there is a glitch here. And the glitch is this: The real, the real objects, the real referents are themselves always the construction of some kind of description, frame, theory. There is never and can never be an encounter between the description, the frame, the theory on the one hand, and a pure unmediated real, real object, or real referent. The identity, the character, of this so-called real, real object, real referent, is itself always already—*as soon as it is named, as soon as it is conceptualized*—the construct of some description, frame, theory.[23] To put it less provocatively, "[T]here is no basis for the subordination of signs to something that is emphatically not a sign, something whose identity and existence would be unconditioned by the contrivances of nomenclature."[24]

The important thing to note is that as soon as reason constructs frames, categories, and operations—this displacement of the object necessarily occurs. The problem of displacement becomes particularly acute when reason is confronted with an irrational object. To try to make rational sense of such irrational objects (for the sake of intelligibility) is in some sense to deny their irrational character (to sacrifice adequacy of reference). By contrast, to remain true to the irrational object (for the sake of adequacy of reference) is to sacrifice intelligibility.

Incompleteness. There is absolutely no guarantee that when critical reflexivity stops one has already identified the crucial formative contexts —the contexts of genesis. To foreground a context within which one is writing is at the same time to background other contexts. To say "I am speaking here as a Harvard-educated white male" foregrounds certain contexts and backgrounds all the others. At one level it announces that one's ethnic character and educational pedigree is more crucial to one's writing than other dimensions of the authorship—class background, marital status, regional provenance, recreational interests, last week's movie, and so on.

The same is true of rational frame construction. When it stops, there is no guarantee that one has successfully identified the crucial aspects of the frame. A frame is necessarily an abstraction and an essentialization. There can never be any assurance that the frame has identified the "right" abstractions, the correct essences. Similarly, there is no obvious way to decide whether essentialization and abstraction have been pursued far enough (or indeed perhaps too far).

For some, of course, this seems like a trivial problem—one that is easily resolved by a combination of good judgment, common sense, experimentation, verification and so on. But this response misses the point: it underestimates the nature of the problem. The problem is, quite simply, that the frame is not simply a tool of understanding. It is more than that: it is the shape and limit of apprehension and understanding itself. If a frame is really a frame, then everything that doesn't fit drops out.

Disjunction. Critical reflexivity does not succeed in fully foregrounding the context because language remains necessarily inadequate to capture the full context within which one is speaking or acting. The unavoidable objectifying aspects of language always succeed in reformulating the context in a form that it is not. To put it another way, the inventory of a form of life (Wittgenstein), a habitus (Bourdieu), an interpretive community (Fish), the Background (Searle), produces only an inventory (not the contexts of which it is an inventory). To begin to try to describe either the essential features, or the genealogy, or the regulative principles of such contexts is always already to transform the context from a way of being into a set of linguistic representations. To express a form of life is not the same thing as to participate in that form of life. There is thus always a dislocation.

Likewise, rational frame construction also fails in making its referents fully present. The frame is always constructed with the available linguistic materials on hand, materials that are not necessarily attuned to the object to be represented. The language substitutes its own logic for the logic of the referent. And it does so in ways that are not easily perceptible or decidable.

Assimilation. Fourth, and this one is really vexing: There is no success that does not end in failure. What critical reflexivity may at first reveal as an interesting insight into context (success) will eventually retreat into the background where it will once again become a taken-for-granted aspect of context (failure). Hence, the first time someone announced in a formal scholarly work or presentation, "I am speaking here as a Harvard-educated white male," the statement was probably thought-provoking—effectively directing the audience's attention to the relations between social identity of the author and his work. The audience might have paused to think about the significance of whiteness or Harvardness as an aspect of context. But through repetition, this act of critical reflexivity, this act of foregrounding, is ultimately retired back into the context. The self-identification becomes little more than the tired ritual of a familiar and boring political code. Indeed, for both author and audience, the meaning of "I speak as a Harvard-educated white male" has very likely become "I speak as someone who routinely bores people by identifying himself in his presentations as a Harvard-educated white male."

In the life of a frame, there comes a time when the frame comes to substitute for the world that it had sought to chart. Its referents drop out and one comes to live within the frame entirely. Instead of serving as a heuristic, a map, an aid to understanding, it becomes an aspect of reality itself—something that is lived. It is no longer the map, but rather something that itself needs to be mapped.

Now, all of this could be read to mean that critical reflexivity and rational frame construction are pointless. But they are not pointless. It's just that they are not everything. And not being everything, they often cannot do the work demanded of them. Both critical reflexivity and rational frame construction are frustrated by the same problems.

Both, as soon as they begin their work, produce a displacement of their objects. (Displacement.) What is more, neither can ever complete its task. (Incompleteness.) And both are always already speaking the wrong language. (Disjunction.) Finally, should either ever achieve a small measure of success, this small measure will ultimately be retired as another banal aspect of context. (Assimilation.)

These problems, of course, are not arguments against reason. Those who champion reason, however, are often rendered uneasy by the admission of such problems. Not surprisingly, what they seek is to find some ground, some device with which to circumvent or deny these problems.

But that, as will be seen, is the way of enchantment. And, it is precisely the denial of these problems that leads reason to develop into its pathological forms.

Activity and Order

Reason, as has been suggested, is a way of selecting, testing, monitoring, and replacing beliefs. Reason is a way of deciding upon what moves to make—what pathways, what relations to create. Reason is, in its various forms (inductive, deductive, analogical, abductive, instrumental, practical), a way of moving from one place to another.

Reason thus has a creative dimension. It enables the thinker to reach new positions. And concomitantly, it leaves behind pathways. In its creative capacity, reason serves to chart the pathways. Out of the materials already available, reason serves to map out the appropriate pathways. As rational frame construction, reason is used to map out new pathways.[25] As critical reflexivity, reason will be used to eradicate certain pathways, to question their use or validity. The question of whether any particular source of belief is helpful or not depends upon the extent to which it enables a person or a group to negotiate its way through the world in the desired way.

Both as rational frame construction and as critical reflexivity, reason requires monitoring of its own productions relative to that which remains unthought. Hence, reason demands that the pathways be monitored to determine if they produce the desired results. Similarly, reason demands that its own information be tested for bias, distortion, reliability, and so on. This sort of monitoring is, of course, conceptually insecure since it is itself always already performed within the pathways constructed by reason.

As the world ages, it becomes increasingly occupied by the pathways established by reason. These become inscribed as more rather than less permanent aspects of the world. They become part of the world itself. Understood, in this way, the pathways and reason itself appear in a different light. In time, the pathways of reason are not only ways to negotiate one's way through the world, but they are also part of what has to be negotiated. In time, reason is no longer understood as a kind of pathmaking enterprise, but rather as an already existing order. The world is ordered in the image of reason.

What is uncanny about this process is that the creations of reason, the pathways, over time become part of the world, part of the unnoticed background within which thought and activity takes place. What was once a creative pathbreaking effort to foreground the unthought becomes sedimented as an aspect of the background. It ironically retires back into the status of the unthought—what Bourdieu calls "habitus," Searle, "the Background," Gadamer, "the hermeneutic circle" (and so on). It is in these ways—both as creative path making and as ordered network—that reason comes to shape the unthought through which we live. Reason is thus not simply a creative activity, but a kind of order—an implicit, and to a large extent, an unreflective order.[26]

A cautionary paragraph is required here: As I have told the story, it is reason as creativity that constructs social and material order. This narrative alone would produce what philosophers call an idealist account— one in which the material is shaped by the ideational. But there is another movement in this narrative—from the material to the ideational. This other movement is one where the social and material order becomes articulated in what we call reason. Reason is a reflection of that which is encountered. This materialist moment is given short shrift here—for it is not crucial to the argument. It would be a mistake, however, to neglect the extent to which reason is a reflection, a projection of material conditions of life. For now, what is important to understand is that the movements are reciprocal.

Both as ordered network and as path-creating activity, reason has certain ambivalent implications. In one sense the transformation of the world into the aesthetic of reason can render the world more ordered. It allows individuals to move from one position to another, to travel the pathways, to apprehend and control their actions. At the same time, however, the transformation of the world into the aesthetics of reason may well succeed in misapprehensions, misconceptualizations, misunderstandings of that world. It is never entirely clear whether certain pathmaking activities or certain ordered networks are necessary or useful, or whether they are instead the unnecessary and unhelpful strands of a reason spinning its own web.

Reason is thus not in control of its own situation. Reason's forays into the world very much depend upon its own prior constructions, upon acts of faith. We are here then back to a predicament already articulated. Reason is dependent upon belief. Yet, it is the activity or the network that is supposed to produce, select, and monitor belief.

All of this creates a rather unstable identity and a precarious situation for reason. Caught within these predicaments, the temptation remains very strong for the partisans of reason to try to stabilize reason.

Constitutive Vulnerabilities

All of this renders reason quite vulnerable. Reason, understood in this light, exists as an assortment of predicaments:

> Reason is used to select, monitor, and replace beliefs, yet it is dependent upon belief.
>
> Reason is a map to guide us through the unthought, yet remains itself grounded in an unthought that it cannot know.
>
> Reason's identity is in tension with its own ruling normative ambitions.
>
> Reason is propelled simultaneously toward the production and the dissolution of contexts. This is manifested often as a tension between critical reflexivity and rational frame construction.

For those who are partisans of reason, the attribution of these predicaments to reason is likely to be taken as a kind of criticism. But that is to miss the point. None of these predicaments should be taken as arguments against reason or its use. Rather, they are predicaments that constitute the very identity of reason.

And because these predicaments constitute the identity of reason, instability and vulnerability are very much the hallmark of reason. To put it another way, reason is very much at risk.

Specifically, it is at risk of being transformed into a dogmatic version of itself. The conflicting pull of these tensions leads to attempts to circumvent or deny the tensions. The result is that reason—as rational frame construction and as critical reflexivity—tends to evolve into pathological versions of itself. Moreover, given reason's unstable identity (its difficulty recognizing itself) it can easily be drafted into the service of even the most dubious and most dogmatic of programs.

Sometimes, reason will simply be hijacked to aid a political or normative program. It is easy to see why "reason" should be such an appealing target for political or intellectual hijacking. To the extent that reason, as suggested, lays claim to rule other beliefs, the capture of reason for this or that political or intellectual project is a tempting prospect. The capture of reason becomes in effect the capture of a mechanism that claims to exercise (and perhaps to some extent does exercise) central command over the selection, monitoring, and replacement of other beliefs.

We should not think of the "hijacking" of reason so much in terms of strategic or deliberate action, but rather as the flow of the normal course of events. Thus, it is to be expected that the dominant forms of social life—whether we are talking about commodity production, technology, science, religious practice—should inscribe their own logics within reason itself.[27] To borrow from Marx, it should not surprise if the things of logic should bear the marks of the logic of things.

The susceptibility of reason to political and intellectual hijacking is all the more plausible when one recalls that reason itself has certain tendencies to evolve in pathological forms: excessive critical reflexivity and excessive rational frame construction. And ironically, we (you and I) are without uncontroversial baselines to decide what would count as "excessive." Indeed, given the constitutive vulnerability of reason, we are even without grounds to decide uncontroversially whether in any given instance we are confronting (1) an appropriate use of reason, (2) the political or intellectual hijacking of reason by some program, or (3) a pathological manifestation of reason.

As this very possibility demonstrates, we should not think of the threats to reason as emanating solely or even primarily from political or intellectual agendas "outside" reason. On the contrary, reason is threatened as well by its own responses to its vulnerability. As will be seen, the very vulnerability of reason leads to attempts to fortify reason by eradicating its tensions, its paradoxes, its contradictory movements—in short, its vulnerable situation. This attempt to establish reason on a stable and noncontestable footing is precisely what we saw earlier in the arguments of Professors Sunstein and Nussbaum. But this sort of response to the vulnerabilities of reason is precisely what leads to the transformation of reason into its traditional enemies: faith, dogma, prejudice, and company.

As previously mentioned, none of this is intended here as a rejection of reason. On the contrary, there is a sense (and not just an ironic one) in which this recognition of the vulnerability of reason is perhaps closest to what reason aspires to be, but can never actually achieve.

Modesty

Perhaps there is a kind of reason that is up to the challenges posed by its own unstable identity. A reason that does not deny and yet does not dwell on its own predicaments might be close to that kind of reason. This would be a reason that comprehends that there are other sources of belief that cannot be dismissed simply in the name of reason itself. This, in short, might be called reason as modesty.

One can, as various philosophers have, simply acknowledge that reason, at its best, is not in control of its own situation. One can acknowledge that reason is indebted to biology, culture, belief, experience, custom, habit, intuition, aesthetics (and so on). One can heed, for instance, Robert Nozick's advice that we see reason as "embedded within a context and playing a role as one component along with others, rather than as an external, self-sufficient point that judges everything."[28]

One difficulty with such modest approaches has already been suggested. The very modesty of the approach, the radical insecurity of its productions, is somewhat in tension with the ruling normative role that American legal culture accords to reason. Reason is the frame within which beliefs are selected, tested, and monitored. If, then, modesty requires that one recognize that the ontological status of reason is no different from that of other beliefs—beliefs anchored in experience, custom, authority, convention, habit, force, intuition, perception, and so on—then it is not clear why reason should enjoy any superior status in adjudicating the value or validity of our beliefs.

And this follows not just as a matter of the legitimacy of reason, but as a matter of its operational competence as well. Indeed, once one takes a modest approach to reason, it is amazing how modest modesty can be. As an example, consider Robert Nozick's concluding account of rational belief:

> Two principles govern rational (even apparently purely theoretical) belief, dissolving the dualism between the theoretical and the practical: do not believe any statement less credible than some incompatible alternative—the intellectual component—but then believe a statement only if the expected utility of doing so is greater than that of not believing it—the practical component. And rationality of belief involves two aspects: support by reasons that make the belief credible, and generation by a process that reliably produces true beliefs.[29]

Now, the point here is not to take to this account of rationality to task for its modesty (or limited utility). On the contrary, the very modesty of this account is its virtue. If Nozick's account seems like a plausible, and even appealing, account of rationality, it is because the account recognizes that reason is a function of context. As Nozick puts it: "To term something rational is to make an evaluation: its reasons are good ones (of a certain sort), and it meets the standards (of a certain sort) that it should meet. These standards, we have said, may vary from area to area, context to context, time to time." [30] Once, of course, one admits the context-bound character of reason or rationality, then the identity of reason and its reliability across contexts become quite questionable—certainly quite difficult to articulate. One is left with extremely modest accounts of reason—very much like the one offered by Nozick.

The problem with modest approaches to reason is that they are in tension with the normative ruling role ascribed to reason itself. Modesty is not reason's ambition. Reason's ambition is to rule. And this ambition is not a severable defect. It is not severable. And it is not unequivocally a defect. It is instead an ineradicable aspect of what reason is taken to be.

False Modesty: The Strange Case of Neopragmatism

It is perhaps because of this ineradicable ambition to rule that the modest approaches to reason often entail a kind of false modesty. The structure of this false modesty is exceedingly simple—involving two gestures. In the first gesture, it is acknowledged that reason has no a priori access to the real, the true, or the good. It is acknowledged that reason is indebted to experience, habit, history, convention, and so on. Reason is, in short, duly chastened. Then comes the second gesture, a tour de force: in virtue of this dressing down, reason is then rehabilitated. In coming to recognize its own limitations and dependencies, reason is now once again fit to rule.

This is a remarkable movement—fascinating to watch—often occurring within the space of a single paragraph and even a single sentence. Stephen Toulmin's account of rationality provides a helpful example. Toulmin is quite concerned to chart a middle way between the imperialism of an a priori, formalist, and absolutist account of rationality and the muddiness of an ad hoc, particularist, relativist account. He opts for a kind of "intellectual ecology" in which one performs a cross-historical and cross-cultural evaluation of alternative strategies in light of the ostensible purposes of their relevant enterprises. He advises that the "burden of rationality then, consists in the fundamental obligation to continue reappraising our strategies in light of fresh experience." [31] At the same time, of course, Toulmin recognizes "the need for an impartial standpoint of rational judgment." [32] And he understands, in some sense, that the two are in tension. But for Toulmin, there is a solution. As he puts it:

> *There is one basis, and one alone,* on which our judgments of 'rationality' and 'conceptual merit' can be truly impartial. This is one

that takes into account the experience which men have accumulated when dealing with the relevant aspect of human life—explanatory or judicial, medical or technological—in *all* cultures and historical periods. By requiring us to accept testimony about human experience in any epoch or culture whatever as relevant to all others, this standpoint of judgment avoids the fallacies that come from allowing special authority to the judgments of any one milieu.[33]

Notice the movement here.

First, Toulmin proclaims that there is one basis (indeed, "one alone") that provides an impartial rational standpoint. This, of course, sounds more monistic than ecological, but let's let that slide for now. This standpoint entails taking into account the experience "in all cultures and historical periods." This is the second movement—when reason and rationality are dressed down, forced, as it were, to acknowledge their contextual character and their cultural dependencies.

But then, out of this recognition, reason is rehabilitated. Indeed, as Toulmin proclaims, this taking into account the testimony of human experience from all epochs and cultures enables the avoidance of "the fallacies that come from allowing special authority to the judgments of any one milieu."

One wants to pause here and ask, as Stanley Fish does: How?[34] Just how is it that considering testimony from all historical epochs and cultures will avoid granting special authority to the parochial view of any one milieu? Just how does this happen? The problem here is not that one cannot take into account testimony from many different epochs and cultures. The problem, rather, is that one will take this testimony into account from within one's own epoch and culture. Indeed, how could one do otherwise? The prescription to consider testimony from all epochs and cultures is all fine and well, but it does not provide any escape from the local conditions from which that consideration takes place. It is simply a non sequitur to suppose that because one is considering and comparing all epochs and cultures, one has therefore reached a place that is outside all epochs and all cultures.[35]

Moreover, reaching that sort of place would be quite problematic if it is "rational judgment" that we are after. This brings up a second problem for Toulmin: in one sense, he seems to want to reach precisely that sort of place. Hence, he considers it a serious fallacy to allow "special authority to the judgments of any one milieu." But if the judgment of rationality is not to be given by "the judgments of any one milieu," then by whom or what is judgment to be given? Toulmin's injunctions to consider history and experience, to make cross-cultural comparisons and to refresh one's conceptual apparatus in light of experience is all fine and well, but following these injunctions alone falls somewhere short of rendering a rational judgment.

Now, there would be nothing objectionable here were Toulmin simply in the business of giving helpful intellectual advice. Most of what he has to say is quite sensible. Most of it is, in a word, modest. But Toulmin is also engaged in another enterprise—one that is not modest at all, one that was announced in the first sentence of the quoted passage: "*There is one basis, and one alone,* on which our judgments of 'rationality' and 'conceptual merit' can be truly impartial." This basis turns out to be nothing other than Toulmin's account of rationality—an account of rationality that is claimed to be not only impartial, but *objective* "in the sense of being neutral as between the local and temporary views of different historico-cultural milieus."[36]

At this point, it is easy to see that a momentarily chastened reason has been resurrected to pride of place. And correspondingly, it is difficult to resist the conclusion that reason's bows to experience, to history, or to whatever other sources of belief were a display of false modesty. It is difficult to resist the conclusion that such displays of modesty were a witting or unwitting ruse through which an embattled reason might feign submission only to regain dominance.

In American law, the falseness of such modesty is particularly easy to understand. Inasmuch as legal thinkers and actors understand themselves to be working toward the promotion and the legitimation of laws, of judicial decisions, reason can never be humbled for very long. It must always be rehabilitated to serve its crucial law-supporting roles. And so it should not surprise if, in American law, claims of modesty turn out rather frequently to be displays of false modesty.

As another instance, consider American legal neopragmatism. A good number of American legal neopragmatists who champion a kind of epistemological modesty nonetheless deploy this modesty to argue for some rather strong programmatic prescriptions. Hence, it is, for instance, that Professor Margaret Jane Radin, who champions a pragmatist "coherence" notion of truth, nonetheless worries (and rightfully so) about what she calls "bad coherence." For Radin, "bad coherence" is the possibility that an account might well achieve coherence and nonetheless display serious ethical flaws. Her solution to this problem is to champion the perspective of the oppressed and the dominated.[37] The problem with this supplement is that it threatens to obliterate the perspectivalism, the relativism, the contextualism, that made pragmatism seem so modest in the first place.

American law furnishes a dramatic confirmation of this point: in the hands of legal thinkers, pragmatism quickly precipitates into some rather determinate programmatic prescriptions. Indeed, one need only survey the rather dramatic differences among the views of legal thinkers who advertise themselves as pragmatists. For thinkers such as Margaret Jane Radin, Martha Minow, and Elizabeth Spelman, pragmatism becomes the philosophical support for those who are "dominated and oppressed"—those who are in various ways other than the white, Christian, able-bodied male. For persons such as Dan Farber or Suzanna Sherry, pragmatism becomes the intellectual support for an enlightened common sense kind of doctrinal instrumentalism. For Richard Posner, pragmatism becomes the intellectual expression of an empirical, scientific, instrumentalist approach to law—compatible with the enterprise of law and economics. For Tom Grey, pragmatism has a temperamental and literary character—a sensibility that does not so much alter one's beliefs about the world as one's orientation toward both belief and world. For Joe Singer, pragmatism becomes the source of support for a Sartrean existentialism.[38]

What many of these neopragmatist thinkers do share in their commitment to pragmatism is what Roland Barthes called "neither/nor-ism." Neither/nor-ism is "this mythological figure which consists in stating two opposites and balancing the one by the other so as to deny them both. (I want *neither* this *nor* that.)"[39] Neopragmatism is neither/nor-ism raised to the status of a universal. Neopragmatism is, in short, neither this nor that—where "this" and "that" can be just about any set of binary oppositions. Instead, it is, as William James put it, "a mediating way of thinking" or, in Tom Grey's expression, a kind of "dialogic oscillation."[40] Pragmatism then is a way of mediating or oscillating between this and that where this and that can stand for a whole series of recursive binary oppositions (including the following culled from the work of Radin and Grey):

reason	feeling
mind	body
nature	nurture
connection	separation

means	ends
public (man)	private (woman)
optimism	pluralism
concrete empiricism	principles
an incomplete dynamic universe	the possibility of perfection
all previous truths	certain new experiences
tough-minded realism	tender-minded idealism
philosophical positions that stress the determining force of material, physical, or biological reality	philosophical positions that stress the shaping power of the imaginative capacity for cultural development[41]

This sort of ironically foundational mediation, oscillation (ambivalence) seems to be very much at the core of neopragmatic thought. Indeed, the neopragmatists seem to be forever involved in counseling against extremes. And as in neither/nor-ism generally, while it can easily seem as if something is being said, it is quite possible that in fact nothing is being said.[42]

Indeed, the problem for pragmatism is that its moment of modesty — the rejection of both extreme poles in any binary — is then somehow made to point to a solution that is just right. In law, the moment of modesty is thus deployed precisely for a rather imperial purpose — to provide an answer, a solution. The raw irony in this procedure is that because the pragmatic moment of modesty is indeed genuinely modest (verging toward emptiness), when it comes time to produce the solution pragmatism can be made to mean or to require just about anything. Not too cold, not too hot, just right — does indeed mean just about anything.

And not surprisingly, just about anything is what we do get. The point becomes clear when one counterposes the jurisprudential views of various legal thinkers who claim the mantle of pragmatism. Putting the views of Dan Farber, Tom Grey, Margaret Jane Radin, Martha Minow, Richard Posner, and Joe Singer side by side, it seems that pragmatism can mean a great many (conflicting) things at once. Indeed, the juxtaposition of the jurisprudential views that claim to issue from pragmatism tend to confirm, as T. S. Eliot once wrote, that ultimately, pragmatism is "of no use to anybody."[43]

Its most discernible content is highly protean — a function of the identity of the person who wields it. What's more, if pragmatism can be made to yield anything, what it yields is often not terribly satisfactory (though it is presented as if it were); indeed, either we get a sort of dogmatic privileging of this or that perspective (i.e., the perspectives of select formalizations of the "oppressed" and the "dominated") or we get curiously ambivalent and possibly self-canceling, normative prescriptions, such as this one:

> [E]ven in the midst of struggling with the complexities of these nonideal choices, we should not neglect the kind of visionary reconstruction that we hope will render them unnecessary. Yet though we cannot do without these visions and these hopes, we mislead ourselves if we try to cut them loose from the nonideal circumstances that gave them birth in order to set them up as a priori arbiter of social progress. We can reconceive our hopes and reconstruct our world, lacking a transformative social theory.[44]

Here we see Margaret Jane Radin using pragmatism to promote an intellectual faith in progressive law—when everything tells her that the conditions of possibility for progressive law have disintegrated. Perhaps therein lies the key to the (moderate) success of neopragmatism in American law. Very likely, its appeal among a certain kind of legal academic lies in reducing anxiety in the face of intellectual disintegration. Tom Grey's slogan illustrates the point succinctly: pragmatism means "freedom from theory guilt."

Language Games about Language Games

Sometimes, in a bow to Ludwig Wittgenstein, American legal thinkers will relax their conception of reason. They will represent reason as continuous with authority, experience, tradition, and the like. Indeed, the more sophisticated American legal thinkers will readily accede that it is not descriptively tenable to distinguish sharply between reason, on the one hand, and authority, experience, tradition, prejudice, and dogma, on the other. They will say things like, "Wittgenstein has taught us that reason must come to an end and that it comes to an end in a form of life."[45]

But even as American legal thinkers and actors relax their conception of reason, even as they perform the obligatory bow to Wittgenstein, they cannot resist adding something more. After acceding that reason in law is grounded in a form of life, the American legal thinker will tell us or simply presume that this form of life is itself reasoned as opposed to, say, irrational, self-consuming, or otherwise malign.

Indeed, when American legal thinkers say that law is a "practice," what they have in mind are practices like medicine, engineering, and architecture. Generally, they are not thinking of practices like phrenology, astrology, or witchcraft.

But, of course, the identification of law as a practice cannot tell us what kind of practice it is—whether it is more like engineering or witchcraft. And, of course, Wittgenstein himself is hardly in a position to adjudicate the question for us. And so, not surprisingly, the neo-Wittgensteinians adjudicate the question themselves. The presumption is that law is a practice and that it is one of the good ones (like engineering) and not one of the bad ones (like phrenology).

But, in making this presumption, the journey through Wittgenstein turns out to be a detour. We have been led through "practices" and "language games" and "forms of life" but, even so, we never left home: we are back to the traditional rule-of-law position. The only thing new is that "the Vienna Circle" has now acquired new meaning. And it is not surprising that we are back to the same position. We are back not through any fault of Wittgenstein. We are back because the rule-of-law thinkers never really wanted to leave in the first place. The rule-of-law thinkers need to retain some distinction like the one between reason and unreason in order to decide what counts as law and to distinguish law from prejudice, dogma, rent seeking power politics, and the like.

Wittgenstein allowed philosophers to stop asking impossible questions. That is his appeal in the legal academy as well: the hope was that Wittgenstein could help legal thinkers and actors avoid trying to answer impossible questions about the grounds of reason and law. And, of course, there are many impossible questions: Is law determinate? Is judicial review justified? [46] And so on.

The problem is that while American legal thinkers want to avoid addressing these impossible questions, they also want to continue giving the old answers. Wittgenstein can certainly help with the first part, but he is of no use whatsoever for the second. On the contrary, the more helpful Wittgenstein is with the first part, the less useful he is for the second part.

It is easy to see why: to call some activity a "practice," a "language game," or a "form of life" does not tell us what kind of practice or language game or form of life it is. And it certainly does not tell us whether the practice is benign or not. Moreover, the very fact that the practice (pick one: law or Satan worship) may have, *as an aspect of its practice,* truly wonderful things to say about itself is of no moment to us if we want to know whether it is a worthwhile practice.

This, of course, creates a problem for the rule-of-law thinkers. If Wittgenstein or his notions of "practice" or "language games" or "forms of life" cannot vouchsafe the activity of law, then the neo-Wittgensteinians are in trouble. They are in trouble precisely because they have just finished invoking Wittgenstein to repudiate such impossible inquiries. They are thus left in the rather unpleasant situation of not knowing what kind of practice law is (whether it is benign or malign) and of having precluded everyone (including themselves) from inquiring into its grounds.

There is another way to put the point: The Wittgensteinian insight that certain philosophical questions are impossible to answer and thus pointless to pursue is itself a local insight. This does not mean that the insight might not be relevant to practices other than philosophy. (It certainly might.) Rather, this means that the insight is one that has been worked out locally by Wittgenstein in the context of philosophy. Its value and integrity, as an insight, indeed depends upon its being worked out in its local context. That means that the insight cannot be just *ipso facto* "applied" or "imported" into another practice.[47] Rather, the validity of the insight for the other practices (say, law) needs to be worked out locally. It may be that the insight is relevant to the practice of law. It is also possible, however, that the practice of law is constituted in such a way that the insight is inapposite. To put it broadly: There can be no a priori, practice-transcendent payoff to the Wittgensteinian insight. To put it still another way: The relevance of the Wittgensteinian to any practice is itself practice-dependent.

Wittgenstein knew this. Stanley Fish knows this. The neo-Wittgensteinians (at least in law) seem largely to have missed the point. Instead, they exhibit the characteristic tendency of the legal thinker or actor to transform intellectual insight into legal authority and to put the latter to work in the cause of law. As much as this sort of operation may be consonant with the practices of law and legal thought, it is not much in keeping with Wittgenstein. Indeed, before drafting Wittgenstein into service as the savior of American law, a few rather large obstacles have to be overcome.

First, with his insistence on the local character of practice, Wittgenstein would have been among the last to suggest that his own insights about philosophy could be transposed to practices such as law.[48] When the queen of the sciences abdicates, when she renounces her foundationalist ambitions, she is no longer in a very good position to counsel (let alone command) that the other disciplines follow suit. You just can't go around saying things like, "Be contextual—always!" and expect to be taken at your word. It's not credible.

Not only that, but once one adopts Wittgenstein's practice-specific localism, there is no particular reason to believe that the epistemological insights in one practice (say, the practice of philosophy) hook up in any particular way whatsoever with the workings of another practice (say, American law). The reason is simple: Suppose that the practice of law, like the practice of religion, depends, so far as the practitioners are concerned, upon the belief in a practice-transcendent conceptual foundation. Suppose that is the practice as its practitioners understand it. What is Wittgenstein going to say to those who are within the practice? "Look here, you people are completely mistaken about the nature of your own practice." Not likely. Now, it is true that Wittgenstein could say such a thing as *a matter of his own practice*. And it would be an interesting thing to say *within his own practice*. But it would be irrelevant to the practice of law or religion.

Second, while Wittgenstein makes a lot of statements relating thinking to practice, one of the things that his work does not do (quite understandably, given his views) is identify the boundaries and identities of practices. Indeed, Wittgenstein quite understandably refrains from offering any recipe or criteria for identifying what constitutes *one* practice, *one* language game, *one* form of life (and what their bounds are). Wittgenstein understood this. Stanley Fish understands this.

American legal thinkers, by contrast, do not. On the contrary, they are not shy at all about such things as jurisdiction. And they know where one jurisdiction ends and another begins. Thus it is that legal thinkers fond of Wittgenstein are ready to deploy his thought to "law." The raw irony is that, while they institute the sophisticated antifoundationalism of Wittgenstein in what they call "law," they are simultaneously—through their very declaration of what the practice of "law" is—reinstituting the very sort of conceptual foundationalism that Wittgenstein warned us against.

At this point, it becomes obvious why Wittgenstein did not give criteria or recipes by which to adjudicate the identity or boundaries of a practice, a language game, a form of life. To do so would have been to reintroduce by the back door the conceptual foundationalism he strived so hard to dispel.

Presumption

Wittgenstein may be in fashion, but modesty is not—particularly not among the partisans of reason, and especially not where American law is concerned. On the contrary, where American law is concerned, the claims of reason to rule are typically pressed rather aggressively.

In American law, it is not modesty but presumption that is the order of the day. Reason is presumed to rule. Its shortcomings, its limitations, its self-doubts are often forgotten. The spirit of contemporary American legal thought is well captured by Professor George Priest, who testified on the state of American legal thought on the occasion of the Robert Bork Hearings. Priest said:

> Since World War II (although there are some examples before) there has been an increasing sophistication of legal scholarship. The increase in sophistication has derived from a much greater focus on underlying theories or conceptual ideas about the law and about rules to govern the legal system. Much of this sophistication comes from the application to legal contexts of social science theories. But the more general development has been the adoption by legal scholars of the style of the sciences. . . . [T]his style has generated a sense of extraordinary competition among aggressive scientists.
>
> The style of competition in the sciences has been consciously emulated by the most ambitious of legal scholars. There remains a range of legal scholarship which, like the typical legal scholarship prior to World War II, is largely descriptive, recommending modest improvements in the law. But the principal development since World War II has been the emergence of aggressive legal scholars, who compete with each other for dominant theories of the law, competing much like athletes seeking records or like 17th and 18th century explorers seeking new discoveries: competing to promote new theories and new ideas around which fields of law will be organized.[49]

Among American legal actors and thinkers, legal controversies are presumed to be subject to the rule of reason. Disagreement and conflict are understood within the terms of analytical matrices. The views of opponents are treated not as the products of different perspectives, but as lapses of reason.

Thus when Dworkin, the preeminent American jurisprude, turned his attention to abortion in 1993, he concluded that the abortion controversy rested on *an analytical mistake*. Specifically, this analytical mistake was the confusion between the personhood of the fetus and the sacredness of human life. Posner responded with acid wit:

> The idea that even the most passionate political and ideological disagreements rest *on mere analytic errors* is the faith of a certain kind of analytic philosopher well illustrated by Dworkin. . . . If the antiabortion people have merely been confused all these years, it is curious that no one was able to set them to rights until Dworkin wrote his book.[50]

This attempt to use reason to evaluate and adjudicate the validity of core ethical and political beliefs is very much the faith of the contemporary American legal thinker. Indeed, the latter is often seen posturing as a presiding officer in the court of reason, ready at a moment's notice to rule from the bench on whether other people's beliefs comport with reason or not. Entire political and moral positions are dismissed on the grounds that they are analytically flawed. Hence, for instance, one commentator simply decides that the communitarian attacks on rights *"is based on confusion and on a failure to make necessary distinctions.* The attack is best aimed at particular rights, not at rights as such. In its usual form, it depends on *a misunderstanding* of what rights are and of what they do."[51] This is presumption at work. Reason here is already presumed to rule. Political and moral disagreement here is reduced to accusations of lapses in analytical reasoning—specifically, to "confusion and on a failure to make necessary distinctions." This presumption is quite prevalent in American law. In part, this presumption is an outgrowth of the rule of reason—the use of reason to select, test, and monitor beliefs.

It might well be argued, of course, that this sort of rhetoric is a betrayal of reason. It can be understood as an attempt to deify reason. It can be construed as an attempt to fortify reason by transforming it into a more stable kind of belief—something on the order of faith.

5 Divine Deceptions

Today . . . we see ourselves as it were entangled in error, *necessitated* to error, to precisely the extent that our prejudice in favor of reason compels us to posit unity, identity, duration, substance, cause, materiality, being. FRIEDRICH NIETZSCHE[1]

They also made mental phenomena into independent beings, their own feelings into qualities of things, the passions which governed the world, in short, predicates of their own nature, whether recognised as such or not into independent subjective existences. LUDWIG FEUERBACH[2]

The enchantment of reason is rendered possible by the very role and identity of reason itself. If truly reason is a web of intelligibility, and if truly it serves to select, test, and monitor beliefs, then reason can easily come to occupy the place of a god. Reason becomes, in Kenneth Burke's coinage, a "god term"[3]—the ultimate substance that dissolves and unifies the manifold. Reason becomes the name for what secures the order of the cosmos.

And in playing such a role, reason comes to serve the psychological and the spiritual needs previously serviced by a deity. It provides succor and comfort. It shields the individual from the chaos. Hence, reason comes to be worshiped as a god and comes to be defended with the blind ardor that the faithful always reserve for their god. Indeed, the aggressive rhetoric of the partisans of reason is reminiscent of nothing so much as the reaction of the believer in the face of blasphemy.

Ironically, as reason becomes deified, it becomes denatured—less and less capable of checking its own operations. It collapses into what it claims to oppose: faith, dogma, prejudice, and company.

The vulnerability resulting from this collapse renders reason a captive to whatever material and social forces predominate. Reason and thus law itself become vehicles for the rule of the dominant forms of life. As I will argue, this means, in one sense, the continued hold of a religious or spiritual aesthetic—the continued enchantment of the world. It means, at the same time, the rule of technology, bureaucracy, and the commodity form.

This is an odd, a schizoid, combination. Like the simultaneous occurrence of stagnation and inflation, it is the sort of combination that most people (until recently) would have thought impossible—a kind of technocratic dark age, an odd conjunction of the magical and the technological.

One result of this schizoid combination is the spiritualization and veneration of the profane and the vulgar. This tendency has been observed in the general culture. What is striking (though not surprising) is that American law exhibits the same tendencies.[4] Hence it is, for instance, that the unfettered promotion of commerce through manipulative advertising is celebrated as a triumph of freedom of speech.[5] The recognition of rights in corporate institutions whose behavior is almost entirely captive to market forces is celebrated as a vindication of human freedom.[6] The production of Kafkaesque legal mazes under the aegis of procedural due process is depicted as a culmination of human freedom.

On the other side, the results include the vulgarization of the spiritual and the sacred. Hence, the techniques of technocracy are applied to determine tolerable ranges for lost or impaired human life. Cost-benefit analysis becomes the regulatory methodology of choice. Damages awards in torts cases, for instance, are determined in terms of percentages—percentage assessments of fault, of causal responsibility, of chances of survival, and so on. The world, even the sacred and the spiritual, becomes *materialized* into quantum amounts—quantum amounts of risk, utility, benefit. Meanwhile, the relations between these quantum materializations are reduced to relations of instrumentality: To what extent does this conduce to that?

Thus what we have is the simultaneous spiritualization of technocracy and the technocratization of spirit.

American legal scholarship, rather than recognizing and coming to terms with this schizoid development, simply reproduces it. Virtually all of American legal scholarship falls within three approaches—not one of which recognizes, much less understands, this propagation of the schizoid. The *spiritual tendency* champions the poetic, spiritual, religious side of law. The *scientific tendency* celebrates the technocratic, scientific side of law. The *conflationist tendency* praises both in suitably specified (or suitably unspecified) ratios while denying that there is any tension between the two.

The spiritual tendency is manifested in the work of those legal thinkers who strive to humanize law. They seek to liken law to literature, to poetry, to moral reflection, to spiritual enlightenment. For instance, the work of James Boyd White, a leading figure in the law and literature school, repeatedly emphasizes the humanistic and spiritual dimensions of law. Sometimes, this humanistic thought is actually used to evaluate and impugn law. Most often, however, this kind of thought is advanced as an unabashed glorification of law.[7] The ironic result is that, despite its best instincts (and often its protests to the contrary), this approach ends up poeticizing the dreary, mechanistic side of law. The poetic paeans to law lead ultimately to a kind of spiritual worship of the bureaucratic machine and to a deadening of ethical and aesthetic awareness. It is in this way that one can find one's self (as James Boyd White does) treating the imperious droning of the plurality opinion in *Planned Parenthood v. Casey* as worthy of comparison to the work of Plato and Aristotle.[8]

The opposed scientific tendency can be seen in the advent of "policy analysis" and "law and economics." Many legal thinkers who pursue economic or policy analysis draw their inspiration from the aesthetics and methods of positivist social science, which in turn draws its inspiration from natural science. Here, too, some of this work is sometimes used to criticize law—but most often in a way that redeems its conceptual architecture and institutional apparatus. The irony, of course, is that all these scientific approaches work with and, more importantly, *within* the fundamental categories, concepts, and grammar established by common, statutory, and constitutional law. Thus, all these attempts at scientific rigor remain subordinate to scientifically unredeemed (often feudal) concepts such as "contingent remainder," "minimum contacts," "proximate cause," "nuisance," "libel per quod" (and so on).

The third, conflationist tendency, is probably the most prevalent in the American legal academy. It is the one that dominates the work of the courts. The fundamental gesture here lies in a denial of any tension between science and spirit. The promise is that it is possible to have both, without compromising either. Sometimes, the denial of the tension is effectuated by the explicit advocacy for a combination of the two tendencies.[9] Much of the neopragmatic literature, for instance, champions such a synthesis. Most often, however, legal thinkers combine science and spirit without reflection—that is, without any recognition of the dissonance involved. In the conflationist tendency, there is simply no recognition that science and spirit, determinism and free will, necessity and freedom do not combine very elegantly. This professional naïveté among legal actors and thinkers routinely yields surprisingly confident assertions of excruciatingly fact-specific distinctions between the realms of science and spirit, determinism and free will, coercion and choice, and so on.[10] To be a typical American legal thinker is thus to be the kind of person *who just simply knows* where coercion leaves off and free choice begins. It is to be the sort of person *who just simply knows* where the border between determinism and free will is located.

In all three kinds of legal scholarship, reason becomes a kind of spirit in the service of the machine and reason becomes a kind of machinery in the service of spirit. What law produces is the enchantment of the profane and the profanation of enchantment.

Enchantment

There is little that is easier than to construct something in accordance with the categories and grammar of one's own time: being constructive is easy. In American law—a field notably exempt from any strong intellectual frame—being constructive is particularly easy. One simply repeats the conventional wisdom (preferably, using a new nomenclature), says things that the legal community likes to hear, condemns what it doesn't, and generally refrains from asking questions that law cannot answer.[11] What is truly difficult in American law, by contrast, is to destroy enough of the categories, the grammar, the operations of the legal mind to gain some perspective on the law.

I know this sounds destructive, perhaps even nihilistic. But there is an important point here: American legal thinkers, as a group, seem to have almost completely lost the capacity for detachment from the law. They are quite able to detach themselves from this or that law, this or that judicial decision. But they seem almost completely incapable of being detached vis-à-vis the law. Detachment from one's object of inquiry is, of course, necessary to say anything interesting about it. This may help explain why American legal thinkers often have interesting things to say about particular laws or particular cases—and yet very little that is of any interest about the law as such. They are detached from and can thus think about the former; they do not have enough detachment from the latter to say anything about it.

There is, of course, one thing that is even easier than being constructive and it too is very common in American law and legal thought. It consists of praising the essence of the law as it already exists. In part, that is what enchantment is about. Here is an illustration of how it works:

> It *seems clear* that people may agree on a correct outcome even though they do not have a theory to account for their judgments. Jones may know that dropped objects fall, that bee stings hurt, that hot air rises, and that snow melts, without knowing exactly why these facts are true. *The same is true of morality.* Johnson may know that slavery is wrong, that government may not stop political protests, that every person should have just one vote, and that it is bad for government to take property unless it pays for it, without knowing exactly or entirely why these things are so. Moral judgments may be right or true even if they are reached by people who lack a full account of those judgments. *The same is true of law. . . . We may thus offer an epistemological point: People can know that* x *is true without entirely knowing* why x *is true. Very often this is so for particular conclusions about law.*[12]

This is the sort of argument that a medieval priest could not fail to love. Here it is again, slightly modified for a medieval audience:

> Everybody knows that dropped objects fall, that bee stings hurt, that witches should be burned, that angels have two wings, and that Mary was a virgin. . . . We may thus offer an epistemological point: People can know that *x* is true without entirely knowing why *x* is true.

Indeed.

The first quote is taken from a somewhat lengthy disquisition on legal reasoning by Professor Cass Sunstein. The quote is exemplary of contemporary legal reasoning. The author simply presumes the self-evident reality of the crucial entities and their relations. In the case of Professor Sunstein, there is no pause to consider that perhaps crucial legal entities (rules, principles, doctrines) might not have exactly the same ontological status as "dropping objects" or "bee stings." Never once is there any sort of critical inquiry into the ontological status or identity of such legal artifacts.

Instead, right from the start, the crucial legal entities are endowed with the same ontological status and identity as "dropping objects" and "bee stings." Later in Professor Sunstein's disquisition he will speak about the Constitution, statutes, and so on as if they were as surely there and in the same way as "dropping objects" or "bee stings."

The Ways of Enchantment

This is the way in which the enchantment of law is produced. Two complementary moments are critical in producing this enchanted world of jurisprudence. I have separated them out here for purposes of exposition, but it should be understood that they often occur together.

The first—*the negative moment*—is basically a failure of critical mind. It is the failure to pursue any sort of critical ontological inquiry into the identity or status of law. Thus, while American legal thinkers will inquire, often in a sustained, sophisticated, and quite critical manner, into the consequences, meanings, value, and formal definitions of artifacts like "rights," "principles," or "rules," they virtually never question the *ontological identity or status* of such legal artifacts. They will presume (when talking about such legal artifacts) that there is an identifiable referent there and that the only question is what to say about "it." Nearly always, they will presume that there are such things as principles, policies, rules, rights, and that their ontological status is not in need of any elaboration.

It simply does not occur to American legal thinkers (and for understandable reasons, much less, to legal actors) to inquire into the ontological status of law or legal artifacts. It does not occur to them to pose such a question because it is no useful part of the enterprise in which they are engaged. They understand themselves to be engaged in enterprises such as "maintaining the rule of law," "preserving order," "promoting progressive legal change," or, at a more mundane level, serving the interests of cause and client. Legal thinkers and actors are engaged (or at least believe they are engaged) in the enterprise of "doing law"—of doing things with law. To the extent that "doing law" is an enterprise of legal advocacy, there is no payoff in any public questioning of the fundamental artifacts that make this work of legal advocacy and legal persuasion at once possible and seemingly meaningful. And because virtually all American legal thinkers are committed (and understand themselves to be committed) to law and its continuation, the questioning doesn't happen.

The second moment—*the positive moment*—lies in reposing faith in the legal artifacts—artifacts like rules, principles, doctrines, values (and so on). Legal actors and thinkers come to believe that when they talk about rules, principles, doctrines, and the like—they are talking about things that are as incontestable as "dropping objects" and "bee stings." Indeed, American legal thinkers and actors treat rules, principles, doctrines and the like as if they were physical objects or mindful subjects.

The apprehension of legal artifacts as object-forms is an instance of

what I call the *objectivist aesthetic*. In this aesthetic, the various qualities that are usually ascribed to objects, to things, are ascribed to legal
artifacts, like rules, rights, and the like. In other words, legal artifacts
are treated as having a stabilized identity—one characterized by substantiality, boundedness, divisibility, extension, spatial location, and temporal location. Some legal artifacts are even gifted with motion and force.

The apprehension of legal artifacts as subjective agencies endowed
with the qualities of mindful life is an instance of what I call the *subjectivist aesthetic*. In this aesthetic, both law and the legal entities are cast as
the effective source of legal action. They become personified—endowed
with the characteristics reserved for subjects: will, intention, purpose,
and even personality.

I call these two forms "aesthetics" in the sense that they are stylized
forms within which law is perceived, apprehended, and expressed. I also
mean to suggest by the term "aesthetic" that these forms of perception,
apprehension, and expression are figurations that precede (and almost
always evade) the conscious prosecution of legal or philosophical disputes on the relation of epistemology to ontology, language to thought,
ideas to materiality (and so on). In American law, the routine rehearsal of
both the subjectivist and objectivist aesthetics yields a certain metaphysic
in which legal artifacts are routinely taken to be object-forms endowed
with certain subjective powers.

Before describing these two aesthetics in detail, a slight detour is required. We must dispel a fallacy and grant the enemy a last laugh.

The Progressive Fallacy and the Last Laugh of Metaphysics

Given the descriptions above (and those to follow), virtually all sophisticated American legal thinkers will deny that they "believe in" the objectivist and subjectivist aesthetic. They will assert, at the very first opportunity, that they "reject" these visions of law. Indeed, they will often go so
far as to say that no legal thinkers really believe these things nowadays.
They will also typically assert that the inadequacies of the objectivist aesthetics and the subjectivist aesthetics have been pointed out long ago
by the legal realists and their contemporaries. The inadequacy of the
objectivist and the subjectivist aesthetic was news back then. It is not
news now.

In a sense (a very limited sense) this is right. Almost all legal thinkers
today will, if asked, "reject" and "disown" the visions of law described by

the objectivist and the subjectivist aesthetic. Nonetheless, the two aesthetics remain very much in place in American law. There are, as I will argue after describing the two aesthetics, two important reasons for their continued vitality.

The first reason is that inasmuch as legal thinkers and actors "do law," they have no choice but to take up these two aesthetics. The aesthetics remain sedimented within the discourse, the vocabulary, the grammar of American law. It may be that the objectivist and subjectivist aesthetics produce silly and erroneous visions of law. That, however, does not mean that law can be reformed, ameliorated, or repaired so as to get rid of the silliness or the mistake. That kind of belief is induced by what may be called "the progressive fallacy" and its "progressive corollary."

The progressive fallacy is the belief that the aspects of a practice (say, law) that are "good" are constitutive of or essential to the practice, while those aspects of the practice that are "bad" are merely by-products of or contingent to the practice. Absent unabashed practice worship, there is no reason to believe in this cheery scenario. There is absolutely no reason to suppose that the good, advanced, progressive, rational, neat, wonderful aspects of a practice are somehow more essential to its constitution than the bad, retarded, reactionary, irrational, cruddy, dull aspects of the practice. The short of it is, the progressive fallacy has nothing going for it other than a kind of faith in cheery scenarios.

The progressive fallacy leads to what might be called the progressive corollary. It goes like this: Given that the good aspects of a practice are essential to its constitution, but the bad ones are not, intellectual effort can be usefully deployed to reform the practice so as to eliminate the bad aspects. The plausibility of this last claim, of course, turns on the presumption that the bad aspects are no essential part of the practice. If they were, it might be difficult to explain how it is that thinking can intervene to restructure a practice while leaving it essentially the same. Again there is nothing going for the progressive corollary other than a faith in cheery scenarios.

Returning to the objectivist and subjectivist aesthetic, then, the problem is that the mistake, the silliness occasioned by the two aesthetics are just as constitutive of American law as the belief that this law must comport with intellectual advancements and rationality. The objectivist view may be a mistake—something that a serious intellectual must reject— but it is a mistake that is nonetheless unavoidable for any American legal thinker or actor who takes up "doing law."

It is important not to overstate the case: when American legal thinkers and actors tell us (you or me) that they reject thinking in this naive objectivist and subjectivist aesthetic, they are very likely quite sincere. The problem is that their sincere belief has no effect on or correspondence to their actual legal thought. It can't: for them to say that they are not being objectivists or subjectivists has about as much effect on their actual legal thought as their saying "My thinking is never wrong" or "My thinking is always funny." One may sincerely believe that one is never wrong or that one is always funny, but believing this won't make it so.

There is a second and related reason for the continued vitality of the objectivist and the subjectivist aesthetic. The reason is that in order for law to exhibit its customarily desired virtues—neutrality, impersonality, efficacy, determinacy, and so on—the two aesthetics are required. In other words, as mistaken or as silly as the objectivist and the subjectivist aesthetic may be, they are nonetheless a necessary supporting structure for the normative vision of law as neutral, impersonal, efficacious, and determinate.

In other words, while legal thinkers will in their intellectualist or theoretical moments seek to reject the metaphysics of the objectivist and subjectivist aesthetics, they will in their normative moment of "doing law" rush to bring this metaphysics back. They will rush to bring it back for it is necessary to their normative celebration of law. One might say, then, that they are of two minds—and indeed necessarily so.

We will return to these two arguments once the objectivist and the subjectivist aesthetic are laid out. The two arguments are raised in advance because the two aesthetics are likely to seem naive and unappealing—even silly. And yet the argument will be that, much as we may want to reject—and in fact do reject—these aesthetics, "doing law" immerses us in these aesthetics.

The Objectivist Aesthetic

In the *objectivist aesthetic,* legal entities (principles, policies, rules, and so on) are perceived, apprehended, and expressed in the same manner as aspects of physical reality (things like "dropping objects"). While this presumption is commonplace among American legal thinkers and actors, it really is quite a remarkable idea, at least if one stops to think about it. The idea is that law and legal entities have stabilized identities that are independent of anyone's beliefs, interpretive commitments, ideology, interests (and so on).[13]

This belief is reflected in a great number of the practices of legal thinkers and actors. For instance, it is common in law for a faculty member to ask a colleague, a partner to ask an associate, a judge to ask a clerk: "What is the law on [X]?" where X can be just about anything and where the law can only be "The Law."

If, indeed, the law professor or the partner or the judge can expect the student, associate, or clerk respectively to find out what the law is, it is because the identity of the subject who is going to figure out the identity of this law is irrelevant. The implicit assumption is that whatever "The Law" may be (something one can argue about), it will nonetheless remain the same whether it is a lawyer for the plaintiff, a lawyer for the defendant, a clerk for the judge, a law student, a citizen, or a law teacher who tries to find it. To be sure, each of these subjects may have different interpretations of what the law is or what it means. And some of these subjects may well be considered more adept in discerning what the law is. And some of them may well have more or less success in finding it. And it is even possible that some of them will "get the law wrong." But at bottom, the assumption of legal thinkers and actors is that even as the perspective may change, the law remains the same.[14]

In all these ways, and more, "The Law" is something that goes without saying. What goes without saying, what is affirmed without notice, is that there is something called "The Law"—something whose reality remains constant regardless of the identity of the persons or parties who happen to apprehend or invoke this law.

This supposition that the law itself has an object-like character—one that remains unchanged regardless of perspective, use, or interest—is what enables legal thinkers to say that the law is or should be "objective." In turn, it is this aesthetic presumption about the identity of law and legal artifacts that underwrites the more explicitly theorized normative claims of legal actors and thinkers that the interpretation of law is and/or should be "neutral," "impersonal," and "universal."

This objectivist rendition of "The Law" is repeated at lower levels of abstraction—for instance, at the level of the legal artifacts: rules, rights, principles and so on. What this means is that legal artifacts partake of the constitutive characteristics of object-forms.

This objectivist aesthetic is described in general terms below. It must be understood, however, that there will be some differentiation depending upon the specific identities of the various kinds of legal artifacts.

As a general matter, legal artifacts are perceived, apprehended, and expressed as having a stabilized identity—one composed of substantiality, boundedness, divisibility, extension, spatial location, and temporal location. In addition, some legal artifacts have motion and force. To the extent that a legal artifact fails to conform to these features (at least, those appropriate to its genre), chances are great that it will be criticized as a flawed legal artifact.

Legal artifacts tend to be *substantial,* though in different ways. Principles, policies, and values tend to have "weight." They can be more or less weighty—which enables them to be balanced against each other. Rules, in and of themselves, generally do not have weight. But even if rules do not have weight in and of themselves, it would be wrong to think that rules are not substantial. For one thing, it is always possible to "add" to a rule or to "carve" out exceptions.

Inasmuch as legal artifacts are substantial, they are *divisible.* The tacit assumption is that the whole (of the legal artifact) can be divided into a series of naturally reoccurring parts. Legal thinkers and actors often speak of these parts as "elements"—elements of a cause of action, elements of a statutory offense, elements of a principle (and so on). This presumption of divisibility is what enables legal actors and thinkers to frame their legal briefs, law review articles, student notes, study aids (and so on) in outline form. It is also what enables legal thinkers and actors to isolate one part, or one subpart, for analysis without paying much attention to its contexts. In other words, the presumption is that the whole is necessarily composed of parts that are at once distinct and stabilized. In turn, this means that the identity of a part is independent of its participation in the whole and its relation to the other parts. It is this presumption of divisibility that establishes the possibility of the rather mechanistic mental operations known in legal circles as "analysis" and "synthesis." In law, these terms are rarely more than technical names for breaking down the whole into its "proper" parts, and putting the parts together in their "proper" whole, respectively.

In aesthetic consonance with divisibility, legal artifacts tend to be *bounded*—having an inside and an outside. Hence the notion, for instance, that something is or is not "covered" by the rule or that some action is or is not "within" the statute. On the classroom blackboard, legal artifacts are often represented in Venn diagrams. Sometimes the location of the boundaries is problematic—but that will generally be on "the penumbra" or on "the periphery," not at "the core."

Legal artifacts have *extension.* Thus, for instance, something can be within the "scope," "orbit," or "reach" of a rule, policy, or principle. Accordingly, something can be a "far cry" from some established rule or policy. Principles and policies are said "to reach only so far." Often, principles, policies, and rules have to be limited—otherwise, one will end up sliding down "the slippery slope."

Some legal artifacts like principles and policies are endowed with the gift of *motion and force*—they "push" and "pull" in various directions. Some legal thinkers have even suggested that principles have gravitational or centripetal force. This gravitational metaphor is, of course, consistent with the notion mentioned earlier that principles and policies have "weight."

Legal artifacts tend to be *spatialized*. Notice that substantiality, boundedness, divisibility, extension, motion are already spatial terms. More than that, however, legal artifacts are given specific addresses within the matrices of law. This occurs as various instances of legal artifacts refer to each other. Some rules are "under" other rules. Meanwhile principles, policies, and values push and pull in various directions across legal space. Legal artifacts mark the limits, the reach or the scope of other legal artifacts. The outline form, which is an attempt to impose aesthetic order over all this jurisprudential interaction, is itself a spatialized form. It is the formal spatial representation of the pyramidal hierarchy.

Legal artifacts exist in *linear time*. Hence, they have a beginning. Rules, for instance, can begin when they are "proposed," "chosen," "created," "adopted," "promulgated," and so on. Rules end when they are "eliminated" or "invalidated." In between their beginning and their end, the legal artifacts are said to be "in force."

In short, in the objectivist aesthetic, legal artifacts are framed in the metaphors and images of Newtonian mechanics.[15] We are so accustomed to the objectivist aesthetic (not only in law, but in common parlance) that it is easy to forget that in this very usage, some very important things are being affirmed—things that can seem downright bizarre once one thinks about them. Indeed, it is one thing to affirm that rocks, hammers, or car engines partake in the object-form—that they are substantial, bounded, divisible (and so on). It seems to be quite another to affirm the same thing about race discrimination law, personal jurisdiction, or involuntary manslaughter. The unthinking representation of such phenomena in terms of the object-form yield some significantly bizarre views on the workings of social life.

On the other hand, it is this conventionally unnoticed aesthetic representation of The Law in terms of object-forms that enables legal arguments to occur and to take the shape they do in the first place. Indeed, it is the casting of law as object-forms that enables judges, lawyers, citizens, and academics to disagree over the meaning, the rightness, and the effects of the law and the various legal artifacts.

The irony (if we put the last two paragraphs together) is that the objectivism of American law is both necessary and yet flawed. It is necessary to the construction of the frames of law and to our own understanding of what law is. And it is flawed for the very reason that the objectivist aesthetic imports into social and cognitive phenomena of a relational nature characteristics that do not obviously belong (i.e., boundedness, substantiality, and so on).

Some legal thinkers (particularly those who are normatively inclined) resist the evaluation that the objectivist aesthetic is "flawed." Indeed, in a favorite refrain of those who "do law" or who believe they do law, the question is: "Flawed compared to what?" This is an interesting question if one is trying to select options within a given frame. It is a very obtuse question, however, if the inquiry concerns the identity, possibility, or value of the frame itself. Hence, rather than answering the question, I would offer a different question in return—also comparative in nature—namely, whether it is better to know that the objectivist aesthetic is flawed or not to know it at all.[16]

The Subjectivist Aesthetic

In the subjectivist aesthetic, "The Law" and legal artifacts are endowed with subjective powers. Just as the bee stings, so too does the law accomplish any number of tasks—both grand and mundane. Rules, for instance, are said "to constrain," "to bind," "to restrain." Principles are said "to counsel" for or against courses of action such as prudence or restraint. Law is thus cast as an effective agency. Law "requires," it "demands," it "obligates," it "compels." Law and the legal entities are cast as the effective source of legal action. And they become personified—endowed with the characteristics reserved for subjects: will, intention, purpose, and even personality.

Legal artifacts are often endowed with *will*. Rules can often be observed "specifying" this, "allowing" that, or "governing" still something else. Principles are often generative of subsidiary law. Hence, principles can "require the establishment of the rule we have laid down." In their stern moments, principles can act in a "forbidding" capacity.

Legal artifacts also have *intention* and/or *purpose*—where intention is the mindful source of action and purpose is the mindful end of action. Hence, one speaks of the "intent" or "spirit of the law." Sometimes, there is an intention or a purpose "behind" the law. Of course, when that happens, the notion is that the intention or the purpose is itself also law. Legal artifacts have intention or purpose in the sense that they direct legal action. Principles, policies, rules, rights, and values are aimed at doing, rectifying, correcting, deterring, achieving, modifying, compensating, and so on. Sometimes, the subjectivity of the legal rules is aimed not at the conduct of citizens (H. L. A. Hart's "primary rules"), but at the production and maintenance of the primary rules (H. L. A. Hart's "secondary rules").[17] In this capacity, the legal entities constrain, restrain, guide, compel, and so on.

Sometimes, the law is even invested with personality—as in the case of Justitia who holds the scales of justice. One can, of course, dismiss Justitia as vulgar symbolism, but to do so would miss a profound point. The image of Justitia symbolizes, among other things, the humanization of law. Among legal thinkers and actors, the law is humanized, much like God was (or is). And thus the law comes to be treated as a real subject worthy, therefore, of respect and even adulation. This virtual love of the law (the "jealous mistress") reaches its apex among those elite legal scholars for whom law is an important *personal presence* in their lives. Indeed, in the writings of some elite legal scholars, one can see an emotive, even at times sentimental, relation to the law—a desire to be bound by law. This sublimation is not unlike the behavior of Catholic nuns who understand themselves to be the brides of Jesus Christ.

The investiture of subjective power in the law and legal entities is, of course, very much akin to the investiture of subjective power in God and his word. The investiture of subjective power in these legal entities—the inculcation of reverence and respect for "rules" and "principles" of law—is thus very much a candidate for a Feuerbachian, Marxian, or Nietzschean critique. The inculcation of belief in the subjective capacity of legal principles, policies, rules, values, and rights is a kind of magical thinking. It may be that kind of magical thinking that is widely shared (possibly a redeeming virtue), but it is magical nonetheless.[18] As for the extreme humanization of law among elite legal thinkers—"the spiritualist tendency"—one can say about their activity what Karl Marx said about religion generally: The more you invest the law with the ideal qualities of human existence, the more you devalue life as it is actually lived. In a more Nietzschean vein, one might say that this desire to be "bound" by law indicates a weak character—a renunciation of life, a kind of self-loathing.

Having said all this, it must nonetheless be recognized that the investment of subjective power in law remains essential to the idea and belief in American law. The subjectivist aesthetic remains a necessary aspect of American law. To strip American law and the legal artifacts of their subjectivist powers would leave them inert, without authority.[19] They would lose their ability to command assent and to inspire respect.[20]

The Roles of the Objectivist and the Subjectivist Aesthetics

The objectivist aesthetic of American law has been much criticized as a kind of hypostatization, reification, illusion, fetishism (and so on) by various proponents of legal realism in the 1920s and 30s[21] and critical legal studies in the 1980s.[22] If the criticism is that these legal entities are cast as illusions, as self-misrepresentations, then the criticism is well taken. If the point is that legal thinkers and actors often draw important legal conclusions on the basis of unnoticed and unthought metaphorical prefigurations, then again the point is well taken. But if the suggestion is that American law can be reformulated without such "mistakes" then the suggestion is misplaced. It is not possible to have or to do law (as we understand the term) without engaging in such illusions. It is precisely these illusions that establish the commonality of meaning, and the stability of frame, that make law (even if it is the illusion of law) possible.[23]

Sometimes, sophisticated legal thinkers spend a great deal of effort attempting to deny that law partakes of this objectivist character. In an important sense, however, this is an argument that they really do not (or at least should not) want to win. The objectivist aesthetic of American law is very much linked to its successful construction of frames. The objectivism of American law (even if it is illusion or pretense) is necessary to the establishment of law as stabilized, identifiable, visible frames within which the legally trained and the laity can operate. These achievements (stability, identifiability, and visibility) matter not only to the operational success of law, but to its authority.

The subjectivist powers invested in the legal ontology has largely escaped criticism in American legal scholarship.[24] Neither the legal realists nor the critical legal studies thinkers spent much effort revealing and criticizing the investment of legal artifacts with subjective power.[25] Nonetheless, this subjectivist aesthetic can be criticized as a kind of enchantment, animism, superstition, and idolatry. Again the criticism has some force. But again if the claim is that American law can be recast without such illusions, the criticism is misplaced. It is misplaced because it is precisely the investment of subjective power in legal artifacts that gives law its authority. Strip away the subjective powers in all legal artifacts, and all you are left with is a lifeless frame—a complex schedule of directives that no one has any reason to honor or respect except to the extent it serves one's interests.

It can, of course, be argued back that the objectivist and subjectivist aesthetics have no metaphysical implications for law—that they are mere figures of speech, metaphors. The question then is metaphors for what? And here the answer cannot be "nothing"—at least not for rule of law thinkers. The reason is simple: To acknowledge that the metaphysics at the heart of law is "nothing" transforms the status of a number of previously respectable activities. To give an example, the previously respectable experiences of "being bound by law" or "following the law" come to seem a lot like the experience of "hearing voices." Again, of course, there is some comfort to be taken in the fact that we all (or at least most of us) seem to hear the same voices. It's definitely better than going it alone. But still.

The short of it is: when the question is asked, "Metaphor for what?" the answer cannot be nothing. Instead, the answer will be "something" and, at that point, we will be back on the pathways of objectivism and subjectivism.

In a different vein, it might be pointed out that the objectivism and the subjectivism are effects of language—a language whose built-in metaphysics cannot be totally avoided. It can be argued that there is no way a priori to guard against such unwelcome and uncanny effects—no way to prevent language from surreptitiously secreting its metaphysics. And this is so not just in law, but indeed anywhere.[26] The point might even be turned against this very text.

All of this, I think, is true. But what makes the situation of American law at once interesting and problematic is that its authority and efficacy *depend upon* the metaphysics established through the objectivist and subjectivist aesthetic. In other words, this metaphysics is not an accidental, a contingent, nor a severable aspect of what we take to be "law." Law is, among other things, *a doing*—and one of the ways in which the doing gets done is in virtue of its metaphysics.

Still, there are some who argue that it is possible to "do law" without the attendant metaphysics. This is a view to which we will now turn—though notice that the outlines of an answer have already begun to take shape.

"As If" Jurisprudence

For the contemporary legal thinker, acknowledging a belief in the metaphysical objectivity or in the metaphysical subjectivity of law is, in one sense, simply untenable. Contemporary legal thinkers are no longer so well insulated from other disciplines in the university that they can continue to espouse such beliefs.

Still, strange as it may seem, it is important to understand that it was not always thus. Before the realists arrived on the scene in the late 1920s, American legal thinkers routinely believed that legal artifacts—principles, policies, rules (and so on)—had objective identities and subjective power. Today, it seems difficult to believe that legal thinkers and actors could have overtly believed such things about law. But it must be remembered that for much of the late nineteenth and twentieth centuries the law school was a rigorously cloistered environment.

As an illustration, consider the highly modulated way in which Albert Kocourek in 1927 expressed the view that legal concepts might well not be objects at all!

> Where does a concept exist? That answer seems to be plain enough —a concept can have no unique position in space; it is not even clear that it has any spatial limits, or indeed, any connection with space at all. . . . That a legal relation considered as a concept has no unique position in space may be accepted in practical reasoning when once *the unavoidable novelty is made familiar that juridical law is entirely a matter of concepts and not of material objects.*[27]

Legal thinkers did believe that legal artifacts had objective identities and were invested with the power to constrain and restrain. Even today there are some legal thinkers who believe in this metaphysically endowed jurisprudence.

If this seems preposterous, consider that for those who make their lives "doing law," it is very difficult not to inhabit this world. Indeed, for those engaged in "doing law," how could they not believe in the metaphysics at least some of the time? For those who do law, it is necessary, at the very least, to imagine what it feels like for doctrines to "bind" or rights to "trump." More than that, they must act, at least sometimes, as if doctrines do bind and rights do trump. It would be a strange mind that could play such a role effectively while also remembering that it is just a role. It would be like an actor who had to play Macbeth as authentically as possible, while also continuously recalling to himself that it is just a part.[28]

In fact, for the lawyer or the judge, the task is even more difficult than for the actor playing Macbeth. When Macbeth dies, the actor playing Macbeth nonetheless survives. When the lawyer loses his capital case and the judge pronounces a death sentence, the defendant will die. When the consequences of role-playing have such serious implications, it becomes, of course, very difficult for the actors not to take comfort in metaphysics. One would, understandably, like to believe that the consequences that follow from "doing law" originate in some objective (stabilized) and subjective (authorized) reality greater than one's self—a reality that is redeemed in the way things are, rather than in shared social conjectures about the way they might be.

The legal academic, too, is likely to slip into legal metaphysics. Legal academics have slightly different reasons for lapsing into metaphysics: They would like to believe that they are part of a true "discipline" and thus possessed of academic knowledge. It is this desire for a discipline that leads them to endow law with the structure, the continuity, the transcendence of metaphysics. Without the metaphysics, the legal academics are just court watchers—journalists of case law. With the metaphysics, by contrast, they are working on nothing less than The Law itself.

But, whether a judge, a lawyer, or a law teacher, the sophisticated contemporary legal thinker cannot abide the supernatural metaphysics that would accord an objectivist form and subjective power to law or legal artifacts. It may be that the sophisticated contemporary legal thinker slips into metaphysical thinking. It may be that when one is "doing law" the doctrines really do seem to be there—there as real limits, real obstacles, real floors, real ceilings. It may be that when the law "speaks" it has a binding effect. But while all this may be (phenomenologically) true, nonetheless the sophisticated contemporary legal thinker will deny believing in the supernatural metaphysic. Instead, the sophisticated contemporary legal thinker or actor will invoke "as if" jurisprudence by saying something like:

> Yes—doctrines do *bind,* principles do *justify,* values do *hold,* and rights do *trump.* But ultimately: No—such notions are not to be taken literally. No intelligent person seriously believes (or has to be-

lieve) that inert entities such as doctrines or principles *do* anything. That would be nonsense. Rather, these verbal formulations are figures of speech, a way of speaking, a series of metaphors.

This way of speaking is a kind of "as if" jurisprudence. In other words, when doctrines are said to bind or rights to trump, this means only that the doctrines are to be understood *as if* they were binding and that rights are to be understood as if they trumped other claims. It is just a way that legal actors and thinkers have of communicating—or so goes the argument.

On the objectivist side, meanwhile, the response is:

> Yes, rules are objectively there, principles have objective content, and yes, it makes sense to talk about such things as "reach," "scope," "weight," "elements" and so on. But, ultimately: No—such notions are not to be taken literally. No intelligent person seriously believes (or has to believe) that conceptual or linguistic phenomena such as doctrines or principles are real objects. That would be nonsense. Rather, these verbal formulations are figures of speech, a way of speaking, a series of metaphors.

The "as if" responses are common among today's sophisticated legal thinkers. But these responses are ultimately dangerous to the enterprise that they are designed to safeguard. The ambition of the sophisticated legal thinkers (and it is not a small one) is to avoid the naive metaphysics of objectivism and subjectivism while nonetheless retaining the frame and force of these metaphysics. This is akin to having one's cake and eating it too. The reason is simple. Let us concede, for the moment, that law is a kind of "as if" discourse. Let us concede that to speak of doctrines as binding or rights as trumping is a kind of metaphor. Again we run into the question: *Metaphor for what?* If the "bindingness" of doctrine does not come from the doctrine and if the "trumpiness" of rights does not come from the subjective power of rights, then where do they come from? Similarly, if the neutrality, impartiality, universality, stability of legal artifacts do not come from the objective character of law, then where do they come from?

The ambition of legal actors and thinkers is not just to avoid an untenable metaphysics where doctrines are magically endowed with the innate power to bind and rights to trump (and so on). Rather, the ambition is to jettison the supernatural metaphysic, while nonetheless retaining the frame and force of its key notions.

So back to the questions. If the stable frames of law and subjective powers of legal artifacts are not secured by metaphysics, then where do they come from? In the attempt to reject the supernatural metaphysic, legal thinkers often say something like "We all just *agree;* we all just *choose* to consider doctrines binding and rights as trumping." They can say this (and they do), but it is a very poor answer.

First, it has the decided disadvantage of not being true. There is very little in the way of what one might consider "agreeing" or "choosing" involved in the treatment of doctrines as binding or rights as trumping. A member of the legal community "agrees" or "chooses" to treat doctrines as binding in the same weak sense that Americans choose to watch T.V. or drink milk. Ironically, here the use of the term "agree" and "choose" is just more metaphor; it is itself more "as if" theorizing.

Second, it is something of a non sequitur to speak of choosing to treat doctrines as binding. If one can "choose" here—in the sense of going either way—then there is not much in the way of bindingness to the binding. The same tension exists with respect to the hold of values. If the hold of a value is a product of choice or agreement, then it may be doubted that it is the value that exercises a hold. In both cases, the authority that is supposed to belong to the artifact—the bindingness of the doctrine or the hold of the value—is transferred back to us, to the agents who "agree" or "choose." With respect to binding doctrines and the hold of values, this tension rises to the level of a non sequitur. The tension is somewhat less acute, but still present in the case of "the justifying principles" and "the trumping rights."

The Transmigration of Authority

The source of the tension of the non sequitur is easy to explain. One can, as many contemporary legal thinkers, and actors do, strip the legal artifacts of their mysterious subjective powers—powers to bind, justify, hold, trump (and so on). But the cost of this demystification is to strip the legal ontology of its subjective powers and to relocate those subjective powers in the agents or agencies who invoke its names. The question then becomes: Who are these agents and what is the source of their authority?[29] If, as a result of contemporary antimetaphysical scruples, entities such as principles, doctrines, values, rights are stripped of their subjective powers, then their prior subjective power must be relocated elsewhere for law to retain its authority. The question is, where?

Notice that this somewhere cannot be just anywhere. By way of illustration, consider if, in a strategic attempt to forestall the death of God, the Roman pope had said:

> Look, I know very well there are no metaphysical entities such as angels, witches, and so on. It's just a way we in the church speak about things. It is a kind of "as if" discourse. Some of the categories, to be sure, are overinclusive or underinclusive. But better to have imperfect categories than none at all. It's easy to criticize Christianity, but what are you going to put in its place? We are reasonable people: we understand that as straight metaphysics, all this Christian religion is, of course, nonsense. It is just a way we have of speaking. But it is ours and it can be put to good use. Trust me. (I have good judgment.)

Now, from the perspective of a believer this is less than a wholly satisfying stance. It suffers from what one might call an authority deficit. Indeed, once the Christian cosmology is acknowledged to be a metaphysical illusion, God and all his subordinates (including the pope) experience an immediate and radical status demotion. Once the metaphysical illusion is gone, the pope's authority dissipates as well.

The same thing goes for law. If, as a result of contemporary antimetaphysical scruples, legal artifacts are stripped of their subjective powers, then there will be a certain authority deficit within the legal system. There will be such a deficit at least so long as the subjective authority is not transposed away from the disenchanted artifacts and reinstituted in some other suitably enchanted subject.

The Name of the Answer

Once the belief in the subjective existence of principles, doctrines, values, and rights is lost or denied, the search is on to find or create or, more accurately, to *find-as-one-creates* a new source, a new site for the subjective power of law. It is in this way that the subjective power of the law is relocated to other mystical guarantors of the "legal cosmology"[30] — notably, "the internal perspective," "careful craftsmanship," "good judgment," "the interpretive community," "Hercules," "conscience" (and so on). These are grand but nebulous entities.

These are what I call "theoretical unmentionables"—those items within a theory which, by virtue of the identity of the theory, one can say very little about, but which are absolutely necessary for the theory to do its work.[31] Every theory has at least one. A good theoretical unmentionable, rhetorically speaking, is one that looks as if it has substance and content—and yet remains sufficiently empty that it can perform any work required to defend the theory. God was the all-time champion theoretical unmentionable. Today we have more secular derivatives: We speak of "the internal perspective" or "conscience" or "good judgment." The advantage of talking in such terms is that they seem less superstitious and yet nonetheless come close to satisfying the contradictory requirements of both substantiality and emptiness.

Consider the "internal perspective." This, according to H. L. A. Hart and Ronald Dworkin, is the perspective of a participant in the legal system—one who believes.[32] In one sense, the "internal perspective" is quite substantial insofar as it is composed of all the beliefs that a participant in the legal system might have about the law. In another sense, the "internal perspective" verges on emptiness—since, indeed, there is no specification of what a legal participant must or does believe.

The same might be said of conscience. Conscience is quite substantial, as it is ultimately the seat of all moral judgment. But conscience is, of course, also utterly empty—for its identity is constituted to escape specific articulation.

Good judgment likewise is substantial inasmuch as it is the knowledge of the ropes that makes any system run. One need only follow rules literally (within any system) to bring the system to a grinding halt. If systems (legal and otherwise) do not routinely come to a grinding halt, it is precisely because those who run the systems have something like "good judgment" that enables them to make the system "work." And yet, like other theoretical unmentionables, "good judgment" is as empty as it is substantial. Listen, for instance, to the words of Professor Paul Gewirtz. Feel the substance, experience the emptiness:

> How to teach wisdom and intuitive good sense is quite another question, of course, and a murderously difficult one. These may be qualities that cannot be defined or taught by rules, and the only effective way to learn them may be by example, by watching mind and character analyze legal problems day-by-day, and by seeing the manner and habit of good judgment in action.[33]

Listening to the words of Professor Gewirtz, one could easily come to believe that "good judgment" is quite a substantial and important capacity. Of course, one could just as well think that good judgment is virtually nothing at all—that ineffable *je ne sais quoi* that one uses to put a name on whatever it is that makes things come out all right.

There is thus an ambiguity built into these theoretical unmentionables. This is an ambiguity that I will describe here in terms of a distinction between "the answer and "the name of the answer."

Sometimes, "the internal perspective" or "good judgment" or "conscience" are simply offered as names for the subjective power (or powers) that produces law. In this capacity they serve a very modest, but nonetheless useful role. Indeed, it is helpful to have names for the answer—to denote what is unknown and needs to be investigated. It is a convenient thing to have a name for the answer. Here's one: "The Desirable X."[34]

Unfortunately, however, in some contexts it is difficult to recognize that a name is just a name. In a community desirous of belief and deprived of its usual object of belief, the risk is that the name of the answer will be taken to be the answer itself. In the legal community the risk is hardly small. To the extent there is presently an authority deficit in law, the temptation to idolatry—to the "reconstruction" of God (or its legal equivalent)—is significant.[35]

Indeed, in such circumstances, it is to be expected that all manner of concepts and ideas will be endowed with the metaphysical substantiality necessary for belief. All manner of names for the source of law or legal meaning will be taken to be not merely names for the source, but the source itself. The name of the answer becomes the answer—and the legal world becomes reenchanted.

Nor is this an accident: if it is to remain a legal world, it must be reenchanted. It must be reenchanted if law is to retain its authoritative status. The short of it is that "as if" jurisprudence does not and cannot live up to its name. It cannot be merely "as if"—at least not if it is going to do the work of law. One does not treat doctrines *as if* they were binding, or rights *as if* they were trumping, unless there is something authoritative compelling us to do so. But all that means is that the subjective power previously situated in *the* doctrine, *the* principle, *the* value, *the* right, has now been located elsewhere.[36]

"As if" jurisprudence thus turns out to be something other than what it claims to be. What it turns out to be is the continuation of the same old metaphysics by other means. "As if" jurisprudence is necessarily parasitic on the metaphysics that it denies. When the host dies, the parasite will wither as well.

But the host is not dead yet—and the enchantment continues apace.

Legal reasoning produces two kinds of enchantment—corresponding roughly to the law/fact distinction. First, it enchants itself (i.e., law) and second, it enchants the field to which it is supposed to "apply" (i.e., facts). The result is that American law is the application of enchanted law to enchanted facts.

When Reason Can't Stop Making Sense

Because the law and the legal entities are organized in a self-referential way, the enchantment of the law yields a self-enchantment. American law perceives, apprehends, and expresses its own actions as the products of reason.

For example, the legislative products of 535 members of the legislative branch of the United States are somehow routinely made to congeal into a coherent unitary intent—"the intent of the legislature." The same wondrous operation is routinely performed on the thinking of the framers of the United States Constitution.

There are two things to notice about this sort of wondrous operation. The first (which has been widely noted) is that it is not at all clear how one can go about discerning a unitary intent from the discordant melange of intentions of the various legislators.[37] The second thing to notice (far less widely noted because much more disturbing) is the unexamined presumption that there must be a "reasoned" mindful source for the legislation.

This last idea is, once one thinks about it, really quite odd. The notion is that when we are "doing law" we can somehow put strategic scheming, seamy motivations, fortuity, happenstance, sloth, power politics, and general human blundering aside to presuppose that the effective source of legislation is a reasoned (normatively appealing) intention. One does not have to be a gnostic to find this presumption rather strange—particularly given all the learning available on institutional behavior from economists, political scientists, and sociologists.[38]

Constantly, the law posits intentions, purposes, reasoned principles, rational policies behind its own actions. For every lawmaking or law-applying act, the law looks for and posits a reason. This relentless search for and production of a "reason behind the law" can itself be defended as rational. Indeed, it can be said that this is the law's way of ensuring that it is itself rational. The search for or production of reasons behind the law serves to ensure that the law comports with reason.

Hence it is that rules are read in light of reasoned policies or rational principles that "lie" behind them. Hence it is that lawyers, judges, law teachers, law students are always looking for the intention, purpose, principle, policy, value, or theory that will reveal the reason implicit in a statutory scheme, a line of cases, a field of law (and so on).

The enterprise of making sure that law comports with reason is itself arguably a rational one. But as it is instantiated in American law, there is a very important sense in which this enterprise is not rational. The attempt to construct law as reason would have to confront the possibility that a great deal of law is itself not reasoned or harbors many different kinds of reason. American law, after all, is a rich admixture of feudal conceptualization, nineteenth-century juristic science, early-twentieth-century functionalism, mid-century procedural formalism, late-twentieth-century moral theorizing, and the like. The injunction to find some ruling reason amidst this hodgepodge is perhaps more than the institutional materials can bear.

Unfortunately, the institutions and the agents charged with the elaboration of American law and the production of American legal thought do not seem terribly well equipped to enable a critical inquiry into the appropriate limits of reason and rationalization. Two major (and related) problems ensue: *pathological asymmetry* and the *absence of restraints.*

One problem is that there is an unnoticed and unexamined asymmetry in this enterprise of rationalization. The orientation of American law is directed toward finding its own products, its own creations, to be rational and reasoned if at all possible. Hence, right from the start there is not anything like a "neutral" or "objective" or "detached" examination of whether a statute, doctrine, principle, or policy is rational or not.

On the contrary, right from the start, law will posit (on the subjectivist side) the intentions, purposes, principles (and so on) that will enable the law in question to appear rational. Similarly, the law will posit into existence (on the objectivist side) the causal networks, the stabilized identities, the frames—in short, the necessary social metaphysics that will enable the law in question to appear rational.[39]

This overstepping of reason occurs in the persistent habit of legal thinkers and actors to find a reason in everything—to ascribe to legal actions a mindful source. This is what Nietzsche described as putting a subject behind every action.

> I notice something and seek a reason for it; this means originally; I
> seek an intention in it, and above all someone who has intentions,

a subject, a doer; every event a deed—formerly one saw intentions in all events, this is our oldest habit. . . . That which gives the extraordinary firmness to our belief in causality is not the great habit of seeing one occurrence following another but our inability to interpret events otherwise than as events caused by intentions. It is belief in the living and thinking as the only effective force—in will, in intention—it is belief that every event is a deed, that every deed presupposes a doer, it is belief in the "subject." Is this belief in the concept of subject and attribute not a great stupidity?[40]

Legal thinkers and actors strive to put reason and rationality behind every act of law (unless, of course, they are against it).

In this habit, there are at least two aspects that are pathological. First, there is the positing of a fantasy subject, a mindful source, an intention, a purpose behind the legal act when it is quite possible that there was no such mindful agency. Second, in the fantasy construction of a mindful agency, there is the displacement and eclipse of the historical subject through repeated acts of substitution. Hence, the historical subject James Madison is supplanted by an idealized fantasy subject James Madison, "the framer of the United States Constitution." Similarly, historical accounts of legislative deliberation are supplanted with stylized, often sanitized fantasy histories known as congressional hearing reports. The law wants mindful agencies behind legal acts, but it wants mindful agencies whose identities are far more ideal and far more trustworthy than those of historical subjects. The latter are often jurisprudentially unreliable.

This largely unacknowledged asymmetry leads to a pathological systemic preference for law—a systemic preference for more law, whenever possible. The implicit presumption is: law = good. More law = more good. This pathological presumption for law, for more law, is ensconced throughout the legal system—in the law-legitimating rhetoric of legislatures, courts, and law schools. Hence it is that even in scholarly journals, American legal academics spend most of their prose imitating the poses, the idioms, the concerns, and sometimes the imperious tones of presiding judges. One gets the sense that when legal academics close their scholarly works with "And therefore, the Court should . . ." what they would really like to say is "It is so ordered. Reversed and remanded for disposition in accordance with this law review article." Legal academics, as they see things, are on the side of the law (and "law" is, presumptively, a good thing). The dominant supposition among legal academics is that law review scholarship ought to provide solutions (read: *legal* solutions);

it ought to be constructive (read: prescribe *more law*); and it ought to deal with concrete legal problems (read: address the world in the terms and categories constructed by the official legal apparatus).

There is a second sense in which the self-rationalizing tendencies of American law are arguably pathological. The problem is this: At what point does the rationalization stop—at what point does or should law stop positing reasons for this or that law? At what point does or should law stop positing into existence the kind of conditions or the kind of relations that will render a law reasoned? This is not a hypothetical problem. With the promiscuity of functionalism, the permissiveness of means-ends analysis, and the multiplicity of plausible ends and intentions, it is possible to justify just about anything as reasoned or rational. What we have in American law at present is an embarrassment of plausible reasons for anything.

The question is at what point, and on the basis of what criteria, does or should American law stop making sense of law or laws? What does or should trigger the tipping point? At what point does or should the Supreme Court abandon efforts to link a law to legitimate ends and concede that the law is simply a product of power politics or legislative ineptitude? At what point should a court abandon the dictates of stare decisis and concede that the social conditions upon which an old precedent were based no longer exist? At what point should a court decide that some principled "interpretation" of a statute, while salutary, can nonetheless not be squared with its meaning, plain or otherwise?

These are questions to which American law offers no satisfactory— certainly no rational—answer. Instead, legal thinkers and actors offer responses such as "These are difficult questions that require good judgment." Or in a slightly hipper, though no more cogent idiom, "It's contextual—these are questions that can only be answered in context."

But given the nature of the question and the stakes, these are feeble answers. For the question is not whether something enables legal thinkers and actors to come to a resolution in any particular case. Rather the question is *what* is it that enables resolution to be reached? Pretending that it is reason is not obviously rational.

The fact that it is all too easy to "give reasons" that sound plausible makes this a difficult problem. It simply is not the case that an examination of American law can yield articulate criteria by which to delineate the break point—the point at which law will cease to rationalize itself.

What we have, in sum, then, is a *pathological asymmetry* in favor of more law and an *absence of restraint* on this rationalization process. If we think about it, American law rarely steps outside the rationalization process. American law students and law teachers study cases—by which they mean that they study appellate opinions. Appellate opinions, as others have suggested, are a kind of extended brag sheet through which the judge gets to report on how well he or she did his or her job. Scholarly commentary, in turn, is a second-order rationalization: the legal scholar is a person who takes the judges' rationalizations and attempts to "make them the best they can be"—in short, to rationalize the rationalizations further.[41] "Legal theory," in turn, consists largely of justifying the activity described in the previous sentence.

The result is that American law represents itself, on the whole, as an essentially reasoned enterprise—even though its rationality (if any) remains on the whole unexamined. This effort of legal thinkers and actors to describe the law's identities and actions in reasoned terms is itself largely pathological. It is arguably pathological because it always already presumes that the objects it encounters are themselves rational. Sometimes the reason of the law is even absurdly comical—as when the law claims that it is reasoned and rational because it requires itself to be so. Hence, for instance, the authors of the famous (or infamous) "Legal Process Materials" once advanced the view that in interpreting statutes, courts should construe them reasonably by presuming that they have been drafted by reasonable men acting reasonably.[42] One could—and certainly some have—found in such directives evidence of law's eminent reasonableness. On the other hand, one could also find here evidence of something altogether different.

From Virtual Law to Virtual Reason

What legal thinkers and actors reason with and reason about is a world that has already been cast or processed in the objectivist and subjectivist aesthetic. In short, they reason with and within a world that has already been enchanted. To put it another way, what is called reason in law is the faithful carrying out of operations enabled by the objectivist and subjectivist aesthetic.

This means, among other things, that those who do law tend to interpret the human world in terms of law's own subjectivist and objectivist aesthetics. Consider again the key traits of the objectivist and subjectivist aesthetic. Associated with each of the traits is a series of operations that constitute what is called "legal reasoning."

Substantiality. Associated with the substantiality of legal artifacts are those processes that help endow and confirm the substantiality of legal artifacts. Hence, for instance, the omnipresent "balancing" or "weighing" of conflicting principles, policies, values, and so on helps endow those conflicting policies and principles with substance. In the very act of "balancing," the policies and principles become substantialized. They come to have a more or less identifiable weight, a more or less significant presence, depending on the area of law (as we will see below). Much of what the law student learns in law school is precisely the legal community's sense of the *relative* weights of the various principles, policies, values, and so on. This professionalized "sense" usually goes by self-congratulatory names such as "good sense" or "good judgment" or, in Karl Llewellyn's phrase, "situation sense."[43]

Boundedness. In law, a legal artifact should, if possible, have clearly marked boundaries. This is not the only ideal, and indeed, it is one that often gives way to other ideals. Nonetheless, boundedness is, other things being equal, a desirable trait. It is no surprise then that a great deal of legal reasoning consists in testing and policing the boundaries. This border-patrol jurisprudence consists in making sure that the distinctions that mark the borders are clear and properly set. Much of this border-patrol work consists in correct classification—making sure that the right things go in the right place.

What has to be prevented is a blurring of the boundaries. This could occur as the result of errors of classification (putting the wrong set of facts in the wrong legal class). Blurring could also occur as a result of imprecise use of terms—fuzzy terms that do not clearly delineate a distinction. Another source of boundary confusion is the possibility of circumvention or subterfuge. Legal thinkers and actors are trained to be much more attuned to this kind of problem than the general public. Indeed, a great deal of what good lawyers know is precisely how various actors will respond or adjust to changes in the legal regime. The response can be adaptive or opportunistic in a way that vitiates the original impetus for the change. A great deal of "legal reasoning" is aimed at identifying and correcting this kind of opportunistic behavior. Boundaries are thus policed not just to ensure clarity, but also to ensure that they are not circumvented.

Divisibility. Two of the most important operations in law are called "analysis" and "synthesis." Analysis is the breakdown of a legal artifact into its crucial parts—often called elements. Synthesis is the construction of a legal whole out of sundry parts.

These operations of subdividing wholes into parts and combining parts into wholes is what gives the law the appearance of an ordered hierarchy in which the whole is divided into parts, the parts into subparts, and so on and so forth in an endless pyramidal hierarchy.

The divisibility is hardly free-form, however. On the contrary, a premium is placed on identifying the proper parts, the proper subparts, and so on. Much of what a law student learns is how to properly separate out the issues in a case, how to isolate the elements of a statute, how to distinguish the various parts of an opinion and so on.

The fact that there is a proper way to do division is what gives legal thinkers and actors the sense that there is an independent integrity to the various parts, allowing the parts to stand alone as it were. This freeze-framing, which is usually imparted *sub rosa* through Socratic questioning in law school, is extremely important to "legal reasoning." It is one of the most uncanny (and quaintly archaic) aspects of contemporary legal reasoning: the amazing ability of legal thinkers and actors to separate out a limited issue for discussion as if it could be discussed intelligently without considering the greater contexts of which it is a part. (In law, this is called "legal analysis," and it is considered a good thing to do.) Thomas Reed Powell summed it up well: "If you have a mind that can think about something that is inextricably connected with something else, without thinking about the something else, then you have The Legal Mind."[44] Most legal thinkers and actors take Powell's caustic remark as a cynical joke. But the joke is real. And the joke is on them.

The effect of this radical division and subdivision is to segment law into "locales" that are not only distinct from each other, but often without effects on each other. This division-as-segmentation is extremely useful to the enterprise of "legal reasoning." It enables the pursuit of policies and principles within a peculiar "locale" of the law, while those policies and principles might be of no moment or even contradicted in a different legal "locale." Hence, for instance, the facilitation of commercial transactions is a policy of various aspects of contract law, but few would think of mentioning it in the context of torts products liability rules (even though products liability law clearly has effects upon commerce).

In a more abstract, but also more important sense, the entire action of divisibility—of breaking wholes down into their *usual* parts and seeing parts in terms of their *usual* wholes—is to identify the relevant frames of reference. Divisibility is what enables the legal actor, on any particular issue or problem, to determine the relevant precedents, policies, principles, the issues that matter. It is the conventional character of the sub-dividing that enables law to produce informative addresses that enable the legal thinker or actor to know "where" he or she is within the legal landscape. What are the local concerns? What general principles can be brought to bear?

Extension. In opposition to the boundary-setting aspects of law, there is the conflicting operation of extending principles, policies, holdings (and so on). Legal artifacts are extended over new domains of law.

Spatial Localization. Many of the operations discussed already have the effect of spatializing the law. But still, it is worth mentioning there are a number of other important spatialization "legal reasoning" techniques that place law "on the map," as it were.

One of the crucial skills learned by the first-year law student (one from which there may be no recovery) is that of "applying the law to the facts." This is essentially an operation of classification. It is a question of finding the right legal addresses for the facts. The image here is that of the pigeon-hole mailbox. The effect of this highly objectivist image is to emphasize (often falsely so) the independence of law and fact, as if the two existed on different planes.

Temporal Location. The temporal location of legal artifacts on a linear time line has no great significance in terms of specific legal operations. The fact that there is only one clock running—one dimension of time—eliminates one possible source for a plurality of legal frames.

The single clock means that for law, there is only a single time frame. The only relevant artifacts and histories are those that can be slotted within that frame.

In terms of specific applications of law, it is, of course, very often a concern to locate events on a time line—but usually this pertains to facts, not usually the law.

Will, Intention, Purpose. Much of what legal thinkers and actors must learn to do with law lies in ascertaining the intention, purpose, or will of laws. Legal actors and thinkers are forever implying purposes, intentions, or wills behind the law. The form of reasoning is a kind of pseudodeduction which, while rarely articulated, goes something as follows:

1. The law of X deals with subject matter X.

2. The author of this law must have been acting rationally.

3. With respect to subject matter X, a rational person would be concerned about Y and would want to do Z to Y.

4. Therefore, it must have been the intention or purpose of the author of the law of X to do Z to Y.

This is hardly a flawless argument structure. Nonetheless, this kind of pseudodeduction is part of the implicit reasoning operations of legal thinkers and actors. One sees it fairly often in cases of constitutional and statutory interpretation where courts announce what "the framers must have intended." What they "must have intended" is something rational and good—that is, precisely the thing that the judge would have intended in the circumstances.

Sometimes, the action of discerning will, intention, and purpose is practiced through a kind of induction. For instance, a series of cases with disparate facts are lined up and the search is on for an "underlying principle" that can "reconcile" the cases. Ironically, it will often be implied (if not stated outright) that it was the underlying principle that actually informed the prior decisions.

Altogether, the imperatives of American law to "harmonize" the statutes, to "reconcile" the cases is the search for a single mind that might unify the legal materials. The importance of this search for a unitary mind is perhaps best exemplified in the work of the prominent jurisprudential thinker Ronald Dworkin and his juris-hero "Hercules." Both are constantly seeking coherence and integrity so as to make the law the best it can be.[45]

Whether by pseudodeduction, induction, or some other means, the attempt to harmonize and reconcile law is pursued by furnishing the unitary principle (or principles) of the legal mind that would have produced such a law. The result of these processes is to produce a law animated by purposes, intentions, and will. To paraphrase Nietzsche: "Behind every law an intention; behind every legal act, a purpose." The result is truly enchanting; indeed, law turns out to be almost always the product of some deeply laudable mindful action. Thurman Arnold (as Professor Laura Kalman reminds) described the process succinctly:

> Originally, the word "trunk" was applied to trees. Suppose later a writer on the science of things in general classifies "elephants," "trees," and "tourists" under the same heading. The reason for such classification is that all three possess trunks. The answer to the objection that the trunks are of different kinds can easily be met by saying that to a nicely based analytical mind, they all have one inherent similarity, i.e., they are all used to carry things. The elephant's

trunk carries hay to the elephant's mouth, the tree trunk carries sap to the leaves and the tourist's trunk carries clothing.[46]

Just the Facts

So far we have only dealt with one aspect of the metaphysics of American law—namely, the metaphysics that result from the deployment of the objectivist and the subjectivist aesthetic. But there is another extremely important metaphysical aspect of American law—and it is seldom noticed. There is within the very discourse of American law a profound, and quite understandable, desire to realize law, to make law real, to make law the transcendent structure of social reality.

What this means is that the work of law is accomplished in significant part through the imposition of its aesthetics on the social, political, economic realm. All that comes within the jurisdiction of law comes to be interpreted and understood within the aesthetics of law. This is the process by which the reason of American law is translated into the currency of fact.

Through the idiomatic and crucial operation of "applying the law to the facts," the facts themselves become cast in the objectivist and subjectivist aesthetics. The enchantment of law thus becomes the enchantment of facts. Hence, we have come to live in a social world whose identities and relations are largely the imprint of the subjectivist and objectivist aesthetic—and all this in the guise of reason.

As if the circle of law and fact—each mirroring the other—were not sufficiently shallow, there is a persistent American habit of arguing on the basis of so-called factual hypotheticals. Indeed, whether it is induction, analogy, or abduction that is at stake, American legal thinkers and actors are extremely fond of trying to derive legal conclusions from the exploration of factual hypotheticals.[47] Along with this preference for the so-called concrete, American legal thinkers and actors often display a characteristic disdain for abstraction or broad-scale thinking.

The result of both of these tendencies is that American legal thinkers and actors seem to be largely oblivious to the notion that their so-called facts are little more than freeze-dried abstractions. Facts are often little more than highly specific concatenations of ideological, scientific, aesthetic, rhetorical, institutional, technological, and other formations. The point here is not just that "facts" are always understood "in context." Nor is it just that "facts" are always apprehended from different perspectives.

Rather, the point is that the "facts" are themselves often nothing more than agglomerations (perhaps unique, perhaps not) of broad scale ideological, scientific, aesthetic, rhetorical, institutional, technological, *and other formations.*

There would be no problem, of course, if in reasoning about "facts"— hypothetical or otherwise—attention were focused on the construction of those "facts," on what has been *packed into* those "facts" and in what particular arrangement.[48] But, the characteristically American faith in the autonomy of "the facts" obviates the need for any such inquiries.

It is through these enchantments that reason becomes a god.

6 The Legal Self

> The decisive point is not which ideas and which values are set, but that the real is expounded according to "ideas" at all, that the "world" is weighed according to "values" at all. MARTIN HEIDEGGER [1]

A law student must learn "to think like a lawyer." In learning this, he or she will also learn that "all lawyers think alike." But, how does it come to be that all lawyers think alike?

The answer is training. Still, what kind of training is it that enables these people to think alike about a myriad of controversial social, political, and economic problems? How have these people learned to think that they should have come to think alike?

The answer is that they have been taught to eclipse the self (their self). They have been taught not only that the law is formal, universal, neutral, impersonal—but much more important, they have been taught to think formally, think universally, think neutrally, think impersonally. They have been trained to empty themselves of bias, passion, commitments. The ideal, which is never quite reached, is to achieve the view from nowhere.

This training is why law students become so cynical in law school— so confident in their abilities to argue for anything. It is also why many (if not most) legal professionals are often considered such boring party companions. It is also why brilliant, in fact leading, legal academics sometimes cannot do legal scholarship without imagining themselves writing for some cause or client. These are all symptoms of successful legal training. The legal thinkers and actors are all missing some essential part of self. They need a cause or a client to supply direction, purpose, frame. Without either they are like hungry ghosts.

Law students have been taught that the universal, neutral, impersonal perspective is the way judges themselves reason; they have been taught that this is a good way to reason, and that they too must learn to reason this way. They must learn to see things, events, law itself, from the single unitary perspective of the law.

Rationalism

This unitary vision is achieved through a comprehensive prereflective aesthetic—which I call "rationalism." Like "subjectivism" and "objectivism" this is an aesthetic, not a deliberate "philosophical position."

Rationalism is an aesthetic in which the self of the thinker is radically separated from the objects it apprehends and from the contexts within which it is apprehending them. This aesthetic (and ultimately metaphysical) separation of the self from its objects and its contexts in one sense endows the self with a radical freedom. This is the radical freedom that consists of "choosing" this position and "rejecting" that one. For the rationalist legal self, the world and the law become a field of possible "positions" or "stances" that it can choose, criticize, reject, modify (and so on). Two things are crucial in this picture.

The first is that the realm of law, indeed the realm of intellectual possibility, is always already apprehended as a field of positions—of stabilized ideas whose value (or lack thereof) lies in their propositional content. The reason this is so important is that it is precisely by reducing all intellectual endeavor to a stabilized propositional form that rationalism maintains this image of the self as radically separate from its objects of inquiry. To put it in other words, it is the content-focused propositional form that ensures that the ideas, theories, models (what-have-you) remain "out there"—in some field outside the self.

The second crucial aspect of the rationalist aesthetic lies in the separation of the self from its contexts. This emancipation of the self from its contexts, formative and environmental, is what enables it to be emancipated from all forces and influences other than law itself.

This aesthetic separation of the self from its objects and its contexts is crucial to the activity of "declaring what the law is." It is this separation, or more precisely, the illusion of this separation that (1) institutes a kind of unified field of law and (2) enables the legal self to exercise control over that unified field.

Separating Self from Object

In constructing a unified field of law, the aesthetic separation of self from object accomplishes three crucial tasks—it *stabilizes* the self as a constant; it reduces various understandings to "positions" so that they become commensurate; and it provides the distance that allows the legal self freedom to choose.

It is by placing itself *hors texte*—outside the texts, ideas, theories, interpretations—that the legal self comes to have the same relation to all positions within its field of inquiry. That universal relation is none other than one of separation. In virtue of this separation, the legal self is stabilized as a single unitary continuous self. The texts, the ideas, the theories, the interpretations paraded before it may change, but the legal self remains the same.

In virtue of the severance of the self from the texts, ideas, theories, interpretations, all of these become commensurable for the legal self. They are all reduced to idea-forms that cannot have any constitutive or disruptive effect on the legal self. They are all "out there."

Being outside of all positions—and thus subject to none—the legal self is free to pick and choose among them. In the unbridgeable gap between the legal self on the one hand and the various positions on the other, we have an aesthetic enablement of the legal self's freedom. It is in virtue of this break or gap that the legal self is free to choose. The legal self becomes the unitary perspective, the lone eye that surveys the whole of the legal field.

Separating Self from Context

Not only must the legal self be severed from its objects of inquiry, but it must also be separated from its formative and environmental contexts. What must be bracketed somehow is a person's psychological or social history—the particular facts of his or her particular provenance. These must be eclipsed, neutralized or "disciplined" somehow so as to enable the various legal selves to attain the single unitary vision of the law itself. Then, too, the particularities of the social and psychological forces bearing down on the individuals must also be neutralized or disciplined. The tasks accomplished by the separation of self from context are akin to those accomplished in the separation of the self from its objects. The self is purged of all contextual particularities and idiosyncrasies. It is thus stabilized, standardized, and endowed with the autonomy to choose.

By severing the self from its particular contexts, the separation renders the self free from all its constitutive contexts. The legal self is freed from all its contextual influences—class, ethnicity, age, sex, education. The legal self becomes stabilized as an essentially empty agent—essentially empty, except for the law that will be poured into its empty core.

This purge of contextual influence in turn renders all legal selves alike. If "all lawyers think alike" it is precisely because they have learned to

purge themselves, temporarily or permanently, of idiosyncratic disposi-
tions or particularistic inclinations. They have learned how to think formally in an abstract and detached—that is, in an indifferent—manner.

Once purged of its contextual influences, the empty legal self becomes
open to heeding the law's imperatives. What the law demands of the legal
self becomes the only voice it hears. And what the law demands always
is that the legal self choose among its options those that the law requires.
In virtue of its separation from its constitutive contexts, the legal self is
endowed with the autonomy to choose what the law requires.

Take This and Choose It

What we have here is a kind of ego-centered reason that frames all and
any possible jurisprudential accounts as if they were all positions that one
could "choose" or "reject." We should linger a little on what makes this
rationalist aesthetic seem so appealing to so many people—particularly
certain kinds of academics.

What the rationalist aesthetic does is reduce the world to a series of
idea-forms—to "concepts," "propositions," "positions," "models," "theories," and the like. These idea-forms serve as intellectual "handles" on the
objects of inquiry. They are stabilized, uniform, transcontextual. They
are, in short, the building blocks of formalized disciplinary frames—
whether that frame be formal linguistics, microeconomics, or law. They
are, in short, the elements of what looks to be nothing less than "knowledge"—and not just any "knowledge" but a rather stable, enduring, no-
nonsense kind of knowledge. Clarity, precision, economy of expression,
elegance are among the cognitive virtues that seem to be served by this
aesthetic.

But this aesthetic and the "knowledge" it makes possible are not without cost. Indeed, the rationalist aesthetic transforms all it encounters into
versions of itself. Hence, for instance, if one reads the rather voluminous
literature on "legal interpretation," the picture that emerges is of legal
selves choosing their favorite selection from a jurisprudential smorgasbord of various positions: formalism, contextualism, conventionalism,
pragmatism, and the like. Typically, these various accounts of interpretation are represented as if they were "positions" to be evaluated for their
merits and demerits. This representation always and already situates the
legal self as a self that can (and should) "choose" whether to be a formalist or a contextualist or a conventionalist or a what-have-you.

In class, the law student is confronted with the same sort of smorgasbord. He or she is asked to choose which is the right or the better position. In the prototypical piece of legal scholarship, it is again the same sort of scene and action: the author will ask his reader to adopt one of the positions examined (namely, the author's) while rejecting all the rest. Similarly, in the judicial opinion, the judge will "choose" which among these is the true and correct expression of the law.

In one sense, all this choice is terribly flattering. The self never feels so empowered as when it is called upon to make such seemingly consequential choices. Unfortunately, there is another effect. The aesthetic representation of formalism, contextualism, conventionalism as "positions" to be chosen by an autonomous legal self already neutralizes much of what these understandings have to offer.

What has dropped out of this rationalist representation are the strong claims that would be made by formalism, contextualism, conventionalism. The strong versions of formalism, contextualism, and conventionalism are not mere positions that selves can take up or reject at will; rather, they are different descriptions of the situation within which all selves are always already ensconced.

The strong version of formalism is that there is an intrinsic order to law that, rational or not, cannot be overcome—except to the extent one abandons law.[2] The strong version of contextualism is that all legal interpretation is a function of context, that there is no such thing as context-less meaning, and that the context always already exceeds the capacity of the participants to identify and specify its character.[3] The strong version of conventionalism is that meaning is always already shaped by social conventions that individual participants are incapable of changing and of which they remain largely unaware.

Choice in all these cases is in different ways (and for different reasons) quite beside the point. Hence, for the formalist, one can no more choose to do nonformalist law than one can choose to do aerial swimming. One can choose to try to do nonformalist law, but the thing is, it won't be law. The same is true of contextualism, though in a different way. Hence, for the strong contextualist one can no more choose to be a contextualist than one can choose to be a noncontextualist or choose to fly. Choice is simply not an option here. The bite of strong contextualism is to describe the particular way in which there is no option, no choice. And for the conventionalist, one can choose to do something including law—so long as one remembers that the "choosing" is epiphenomenal, resting on the convention to do the actual work, the actual selection.

Now the point is not that any of these understandings are right or true. Rather, the point is that within the rationalist aesthetic, these understandings never register. They are never encountered. On the contrary, the rationalist aesthetic always already envelops these understandings within its own predeliberative representation of the field and of the self. That is to say that formalism, contextualism, conventionalism, and the like are all laid out before the legal self so that it might choose one and reject the others.

The result is that this rationalist self homogenizes intellectual (and other) encounters within the matrix of rationalist aesthetics. Every intellectual current or insight that this self encounters is always already processed and reformulated within this rationalist aesthetic.

That this kind of aesthetic should be prevalent within the legal community is not surprising. This particular framing of the self as one that "chooses" its "positions" is isomorphic with the situation of the appellate judge who, aided by reason, "chooses" among the "positions" offered by the competing litigants. Indeed, this aesthetic is implicit, as we saw earlier, in the very idea of the rule of law and the rule of reason.

This Is Not a Stop Sign

Not only does the rationalist aesthetic produce a distortion of possible jurisprudential and social understandings, but it leads to a rather odd, albeit common, rhetoric in which the legal thinker proffers normative arguments in favor of or against positions presuming that (1) there is a meaningful choice to be made and (2) that making the choice the right way somehow has important consequences. At times these presumptions may be warranted. At other times, they can seem downright bizarre. What is interesting about this rhetoric is that, among the legally trained, it is deployed almost automatically—that is, almost regardless of context.

In legal academic circles, it is increasingly the moral and political arguments that matter: What goods or evils can be shown to follow from this or that course of action? The prevalence of moral and political argument is so great that it is now often considered unnecessary to argue against the truth of a position in order to dispose of it. Instead, it is considered sufficient to point out that the position would have bad consequences or that it has bad associations. As an example, Professor Suzanna Sherry summarily dismisses what she calls "epistemological pluralism" of postmodernism with the following flourish: "The primary problem with epistemological pluralism is that there is no way to resolve disputes between epistemologies except by recourse to power. In this, a regime of epistemological pluralism resembles the hostile religious pluralism—and religious warfare—that prevailed before the Enlightenment."[4] The structure of the argument is reminiscent of magical thinking. "I do not like *X*. Come to think of it, *X* has bad consequences. Therefore, *X* is wrong." And in fact, the author's own words track fairly well with magical thinking. She writes that she is not addressing "whether the Enlightenment reliance on reason and empiricism is in fact the only epistemology, but whether we ought to proceed *as if it were,* at least in the public arena."[5] To this question, she answers an emphatic "yes." Given that she has forsaken any claim that the Enlightenment epistemology is more true or more valid, one is left wondering just what supports this "yes"? Her answer, it turns out, is that it is more prudent to follow Enlightenment reason than postmodern epistemologies. And in a quip she adds, "[T]o act on the postmodern insights would be 'like saying that, since philosophers are still debating Descartes epistemology, one need not take notice of traffic signals in the meantime.' "[6] Now, there is a point here.

And I agree. If you have to consult Derrida at stop signs, this is not good. (Note that if you had to consult Descartes, that would not be reassuring either.) Her point, however, is that in public life, one should choose the more prudent epistemology. Of course, how one tells which epistemology is more prudent without relying on *some* truth claim remains a mystery, but let's let that slide. The question I want to ask is this: One can understand why prudence is required at a stop sign. But why is prudence required in legal scholarship?

The answer is that the author is concerned about the direction of the law. She believes that we are at an important jurisprudential intersection where we have to "choose" between different positions: Enlightenment reason and epistemological pluralism. And so she marshals her arguments.

She is, as lawyers say, "on the brief." She is writing the brief for reason. She is "doing law." The client is reason and she is her attorney and. . . . But there is a problem here. This is not a courtroom. She is not a lawyer arguing a case. And the reader is not a judge. This is a law review article. She is a law professor. And the reader—at least the prototypical reader— is very probably just another law professor. So what had at first seemed like such a common sense, down-to-earth argument in favor of Enlightenment reason turns out to be *predicated on a rather fantastic narrative premise*. That narrative premise is that somehow the author is a lawyer representing reason before an imagined tribunal. And true to form the article closes with the equivalent of a *legal brief's prayer for relief*: "The dangers that the epistemology of the Enlightenment gradually defeated remain very real, ready to reappear as soon as reason sleeps. Lest we fall prey to Goya's monsters, let us affirm that the Enlightenment project is not, in either sense of the word, finished—neither completed nor defeated."[7] Just how is one supposed to respond to this? "The motion is hereby granted and affirmed." "Hey, I'm with you. Where do I sign up?" One sound response might be to wonder just how someone so obviously sincere in her commitment to reason could have been led so far astray. Just how is it that someone comes to praise reason and yet does little but bury it (over and over again)?

False Empowerment

One of the charming things about the rationalist aesthetic (at least, for its practitioners) is that it is extremely flattering to the self. The legal self is endowed with autonomy and self-direction—freed from its context and its objects. Meanwhile the law and the world are laid about before it as a series of "concepts," "propositions," "positions," "models," "theories"— all to be "chosen" or "rejected."

Moreover, the argument in favor of or against these positions is typically addressed to the legal self. Any legal claim must be supported by reasons—where reason often means little more than giving reasons as to why the rationalist self should adopt or reject this or that position. It is in this way that rationalism fashions a self that understands itself to be an autonomous, self-directing, coherent agency that chooses its positions. Not surprisingly, it rarely dawns on the rationalist self that it is itself a construction of aesthetics, of rhetoric, of narrative—in short, of unexamined (and when one thinks about it, nonrational, perhaps even irrational) formations.

And it is precisely the nonrational (or irrational) aesthetic of this kind of self that leads it to write law review articles in order to give like-minded selves reasons to stick with the "Enlightenment project" and to "be cautious before *jettisoning* the worldview that has brought us this far."[8]

The fantasy aspects of this kind of scholarship becomes manifest when one considers the assumptions that must be made in order to render such writing plausibly rational on its own terms:

1. Enlightenment reason and postmodern epistemology reduce to certain identifiable *positions.*

2. Whether or not one adopts either of these positions depends a great deal on the normative arguments in favor of or against either of these positions—as opposed to, say, historical, sociological, epistemic, ontological, hermeneutic, or other kinds of argument (leaving aside the nonconceptual orders of experience, habit, tradition, power, practice, and so on).

3. The self generally *chooses* its own epistemic orientation toward the world by, in turn, *choosing* the best epistemology, which, in turn, is generally *chosen* on the basis of normative considerations addressed to the self.

4. There is now (at this point in time, today, this year, in the nineties) an important normative choice to be made between the positions known as Enlightenment reason and postmodern epistemology. It is important, in other words, to choose one now. This is the right time to do it.

5. The outcome of this choice will have some regulative significance for the cognitive processes of readers. Thus, readers choosing in favor of Enlightenment reason are likely soon to exhibit Enlightenment thinking (forsaking all others). By contrast, readers choosing postmodernism will soon exhibit postmodern thinking (forsaking all others). In short, the mind legislates its own cognitive operations, at least to a significant extent. Once you decide how to think about something, that's it, the decision is made, and all cognitive operations just fall into place until the next high-order command decision about how to think.

6. The readers of law reviews are, given their number and character, the kinds of readers likely to have a significant impact on the future of Western civilization—most specifically, whether Western civilization goes the Enlightenment route or becomes postmodern or worse. Their choice is thus important.

7. (And so on.)

Please note two things about these beliefs.

First, in the context of turn-of-the-twenty-first-century intellectual life, these beliefs are rather strange. For instance, it is strange for turn-of-the-twenty-first-century intellectuals to believe that epistemic orientations are (1) chosen (2) on the basis of epistemological theories that are themselves (3) chosen (4) on the basis of normative concerns.

Second, in the context of American legal thought, these kinds of beliefs are not strange at all. In American legal thought, the kinds of assumptions made above are routine, indeed required. If anything is strange or unusual, it is instead to question these beliefs. Usually, in American legal thought these beliefs are just taken as simply true. And indeed, few are the people in American legal academic life who have ever gone wrong overestimating the power of normative argument.

Free to Be Framed

And, in a sense, this is not surprising. Consider where these beliefs come from. It is not difficult to tell. They are instances of the rationalist aesthetic. In turn, the rationalist aesthetic is the aesthetic of the judge. The judge is given a limited number of positions—often just two—from which she must choose. These positions are not her positions, but rather the positions of the litigants. These positions are out there. She must choose between them, and she must do so in a normatively competent manner. That is to say, she must free herself from her contexts—formative and environmental.[9] Guided only by law and reason she must choose on the basis of reasons.

This is the way legal thinkers and actors present themselves and their thinking. And, like the judge, they present themselves as doing the work of reason. And so, like judges, they are constantly "choosing" this or that and giving their reasons.

The ironic status of this construction of the self is that it is itself not "chosen" but rather framed. The significance of this irony is that it is difficult for this kind of self to recognize that it has been framed. Nonetheless, this is a self that is driven to go through the world interpreting intellectual (and other) experience as calling for a "choice" among competing "positions." Ironically, *that* particular habit is not a choice on its part, but rather something it is driven to do over and over again—almost regardless of context.

Dominance and Submission

In the rationalist aesthetic, the self is put in control and the world and the law are stabilized into positions for it to choose. The divisions and subdivisions of doctrinal law and all those moving principles and pressing policies are all before it. But where is the legal self? What is its ground?

The omnipresence of the objectivist and subjectivist aesthetic in American law produces a rather interesting situation for the legal thinker and actor. To the extent that the legal thinker or actor is conscious of the objectivist and subjectivist aesthetics, he or she can "choose" to deploy one aesthetic or the other. In other words, the legal thinker or actor can "choose" to frame law in an objectivist aesthetic or instead "choose" to submit to its subjectivist commands.

If the legal thinker or actor "chooses" the objectivist aesthetic, he or she assumes a position of dominance vis-à-vis the law or the legal artifacts. The law is there—inert, just like an object—and it is for the legal thinker or actor to do something with it, to invest it with life, direction, meaning. In this orientation, the legal thinker or actor becomes the master of the law or the legal artifact.

Pushed to its limit, this becomes a problematic stance. It is the stance of a self that is outside the text—outside all positions, ideas, theories, interpretations. It is the stance of a self that is radically free. But now, that freedom becomes a problem: If that self is radically free, then how is it to be restrained and constrained to follow the law? This problem of determining what constrains and restrains the legal self—the problem of the *errant judge* and the *lawless lawmaker*—is one that has occupied and perplexed American legal thought for many generations and remains, to this day, unresolved.[10]

The idea of the legal self simply choosing the objectivist aesthetic is inadequate for those who wish to believe in the rule of law and the rule of reason. Alone, it is inadequate very simply because it institutes the legal self (rather than the law) as the origin, as the author of the law. This legal self is, in virtue of its radical freedom, not only not the law, but not much of anything.

If the legal thinker or actor "chooses" the subjectivist aesthetic, he or she assumes a position of submission vis-à-vis the law or the legal artifacts. In this attitude, the law is animated. It comes alive and not only speaks to but commands the legal thinker or actor. In this orientation, the legal thinker or actor waits to hear from his juridical divinity.

This is not an adequate stance or orientation either. The problem with this orientation is that it is not a true submission, but rather a simulated submission. For the attitude here is of "choosing to submit." And that, of course, entails the possibility at any time of choosing not to submit. This places in question not only the general fact of submission, but indeed, the specific content of what it is that the legal thinker or actor has submitted to. If one chooses to submit to law, what guarantee or indeed evidence is there that the commandments one hears are those of law and not those one has chosen?

Neither the choice of dominance nor the choice of submission are adequate orientations for the rule of law. The former supplants the rule of law by the rule of the free (and empty) legal self. The latter is not a submission at all.

The discussion thus far has proceeded on the supposition that the legal thinker or actor "chooses" one aesthetic or the other. This experience of making such a choice may sometimes happen to legal thinkers and actors. But most often legal thinkers and actors are simply acting or thinking within the aesthetics in a fairly automatic way—that is, in a passive way. Whether dominant or submissive, it often seems that the legal self has become one or the other, not so much by "choice," but rather by being framed that way.

Here again we have a paradox: this time with dominance as opposed to submission. What does it mean to say that a legal thinker or actor is placed in a dominant position vis-à-vis law? If he or she has been placed by something else, this is hardly an unequivocally dominant position.

Meanwhile, if the legal self is placed in a submissive posture vis-à-vis the law, then when is the faculty of judgment exercised? It would seem that the unconscious submission of the legal self to the law would represent an automatic law—one lacking in mindful attention.

This is all very disorienting. How does the self of the legal thinker or actor deal with all this? First, a clarification is in order: pure subjectivism and pure objectivism are never possible. The law and the legal artifacts are themselves always cast in both subjectivist and objectivist aesthetics. The result is that the legal self is always at once both dominant and submissive. The legal self is at once a servant of the law and yet also its judge.

This, of course, is a dissonant orientation. Yet, most of the time, legal thinkers and actors do not perceive the dissonance. Within the complexity of law—its layers of directives and imperatives—the legal self finds itself master of some law and servant of other law. Thus, when the legal self deals with law as an object-form and begins to manipulate, direct, redirect, transform, extend, or restrict some piece of law, it is always in response to some higher law, some superior norm, some paramount imperative. Similarly, whenever the legal self finds itself subject to some imperative or command, it is almost always an imperative or a command to manufacture or transform other law. The dissonance implicit in a legal self that is both dominant and submissive is thus handled by situating the self at some determinable point in the hierarchical layers of law.[11] The legal self is thus dominant with regard to any law inferior to its position and submissive to any law that is superior to its position.

When one is facing a concrete legal problem, the dissonance thus seems to disappear because the legal self is located (or locates itself) at a distinct point in the hierarchy of law. But the sense that there is no dissonance is itself illusory. The absence of dissonance is itself a trick effect of the objectivist picture of law as a series of hierarchical layers and of the subjectivist determinations of the location of the self.

To put it in plain language, it is things like the imperative to good judgment or common sense or "situation sense" or the pull of values or moral principles that enable the self to locate itself or be located somewhere within the legal hierarchy. And it is the fact that the legal self experiences law in the objectivist imagery and metaphors of a hierarchical layers of law that allow the legal self to locate itself (or to be located) at a particular point in the hierarchical layers of law. But the fact remains that the legal self could find itself (or situate itself) anywhere in the hierarchy. It is only through the objectivist framings and subjectivist determinations that the legal self comes to be located at any particular point. The irony is that these determinations remain themselves not determined—at least not by any articulate law.

This aesthetic understanding of the predicaments of the legal self is rarely noticed and rarely understood by legal thinkers and actors. Indeed, in order to do their work, they need not to understand this—for to understand this point is to recognize the chaos that permeates the law.

Nonetheless, this aesthetic predicament manifests itself explicitly in conflicting orientations to law that can mature into paradox. Hence, for instance, Arthur Leff argued that in the realm of moral law, we want both to be absolutely bound to a higher power and also to be absolutely free to choose what we want.[12] In the realm of legislation, our legislative bodies must be free to make the laws, but they must conform with the law. In adjudication, we want our judges to be absolutely restrained by the law and yet we also want to accord them the absolute authority to judge what the law is.

Our most common solution for these paradoxes is to distinguish the law that we "choose," are "free to make," "can authoritatively declare" from the law to which we are "absolutely bound," must "conform with," must be "absolutely constrained by." If, in all these instances, these are two different kinds of law, then the paradoxes vanish. But it is not clear that we can effectuate such a distinction in a stable manner.

Paradoxes, we know, are born of self-referentiality. The problem with law is that it is vigorously self-referential—and also vigorously ambivalent in its self-apperception. Indeed, the law is constantly shifting in its reference to itself as subject and object. And it is constantly shifting in its description of the appropriate role of the legal self as subject and object.

Where does this leave the legal self? For the legal self who is most rational and most aware of her legal environment, all this should leave her rather confused. It ought to leave the legal self with the sense that she doesn't know whether she is coming or going—whether she is doing things to law or instead hearing legal voices. Any objectified vision of law can always flip into a subjectified vision. Any subjectified vision of law can always flip into an objectified vision. This doesn't mean that the flipping will in any given instance be persuasive, nor that it can be done at will. Rather, to some indeterminate extent, the legal self has control over this flipping and to some indeterminate extent, it does not.

One would think that these predicaments would be very confusing to the legal self. But the fact is, for most legal thinkers and actors, they are not. The legal self accepts this situation, finds it rational. How does this come to be? The answer is that the play of dominance and submission is stabilized through the dogmatic forms of belief known as "good judgment" and "common sense" and so on. These beliefs intercede to stabilize the play of dominance and submission.

That is not to say that the law becomes coherent in any deep sense. It is to say, however, that at any particular point in time, within a given legal community of like-minded people—stabilization is achieved. The legal self is located at a particular point within the force fields of law. This stabilization is what enables a distinction between the law that the self governs and the law that governs the self.

The play of dominance and submission are key aspects of the experience of the legal self. Indeed, among the legally trained, the alternating experience of dominance and submission is a common one—and not soon forgotten.

The first-year law student, the law review note writer, or the junior associate writing her first brief often experiences the cases and the legal authorities as weighty obstacles to her argument. The legal authorities bear down on her. She must conform to their commands and, without offending them, somehow weave her way respectfully to the desired result. The law is above, oppressive—indeed, very much like "a brooding omnipresence in the sky." She is afraid of making a mistake, of misreading the precedent, of lacking good judgment, of being caught up short by the law. The tribunal, the judge, the supervising partner, is a hostile other—always ready to hone in on the weakness, the flaw, the error. The potential for humiliation is never far away.

This is what submission feels like.

There is, of course, a different experience of law. It is the experience that is gained once one has drafted many briefs, written many articles or opinions. This is the experience of saying what one wants to say and then arranging the legal authorities to support one's views. In this posture, one is above law: the precedents are there to be manipulated. The legal authorities are there to be used. The law appears not so much as obstacle or maze—but instead, as supporting accouterments. Cases are props. The law is just so much scenery. As for the tribunal, the judge, the most senior partner, they are juris-puppets—inconsequential others to be manipulated. They are a passive crew—bit actors who will play the part one has scripted for them.

This is what dominance feels like.

However one understands dominance and submission—politically, culturally, psychologically—the failure to recognize its omnipresence in American law and legal thought is an important failing of the discipline. What is involved, in short, is a kind of cognitive deficit.

For those in the legal academy who wish to "do law," this cognitive deficit is not remediable. It is not remediable precisely because the cognitive deficit is a constitutive aspect of American law. If American law "works" as they say, it is because those who "do it" routinely pursue certain kinds of questions and concerns while routinely failing to pursue others. To put it plainly: To be really good at "doing law," one has to have serious blind spots and a stunningly selective sense of curiosity.[13] If all lawyers think alike (a nice way of saying they lack imagination) it is precisely because our very idea of "law" requires that they think alike. It demands that when they look at "the law" they see just one thing—and if at all possible, the same thing. This is no small achievement. It is nothing to sneer at. At the same time, it would be surprising if it were without cost.

Epilogue: Reason without End

Recall the police search in "The Purloined Letter." Imagine being part of the police. Imagine going from room to room, compartment to compartment, following the program. Imagine doing this repeatedly, endlessly. Imagine getting nowhere—achieving nothing.

Boring and Dreary/Dreary and Boring

Like the police search in "The Purloined Letter," a great deal of legal work is excruciatingly boring. One need only pick up a judicial opinion, a state statute, a federal regulation, or a law review article to experience an overwhelming sense of dread and ennui.

For the legally trained, part of the boredom stems from the familiarity of the grids, the moves, the operations. The sense is omnipresent that there really is nothing new. The only thing that is novel is the specific arrangement of authoritative legal artifacts (statutes, cases, whatever) that form the focus of attention. Perhaps there are some who continue to find intellectual interest manipulating the canonical materials in the approved ways. But to find meaning or interest in these canonical materials requires an impoverished imagination. And in a sense that is precisely the way American law does its work: it impoverishes the imagination of legal professionals so as to produce homogeneous meanings. That is the way law constitutes itself as law.

The dreariness of déja vu might be tolerable if one could muster the sense that the countless normative prescriptions contained in judicial opinions, statutes, regulations, and law review articles mattered. But by and large they don't.

It's not happening. One could, I suppose, sustain a lively interest in this Sisyphean enterprise if one were convinced that it was an aesthetically appealing form of life. But, by and large, it is not. It is dreary and boring. And while boredom does not rank high in the emotional register, it is not something to be ignored. Boredom has a social aspect. Specifically, boredom is the emotional response to the continued dominance of a social form that has lost its vitality.

To put it simply, boredom is a symptom of nihilism.

Nihilism

Nihilism is the modern charge typically issued by the faithful against the heretics. In this capacity, it is often a woefully inappropriate epithet or diagnosis. It is inappropriate precisely because the dissidents are, for good or ill, typically much more passionate in their beliefs than the faithful. Indeed, if heretics suffer from a pathology of belief, it is usually excessive zeal and passion (not nihilism).

Nihilism—Heidegger would call it "weak nihilism"—is much more a pathology of the orthodoxy. What produces nihilism is precisely the continuation of a form of belief once it has lost its vitality. Nihilism is the willful continuation of the belief once it can no longer command respect or inspire commitment.

This is very much the state of American law: what we have is a group of thinkers and actors who no longer respect their grid, who no longer believe in its operations, but who also have not the slightest idea what else to do. They have very nice positions—both morally and professionally—and they are incapable of giving them up.

And so they continue to say nice things to power. They police the grid; they run the mazes. After a while, it is the other way around.

Life in the Grid—Running the Mazes

When rationalism is in place, experience, perception, awareness, reflection, tradition are recast in the image of reason or they are relegated to a secondary supporting status where they serve to confirm what reason has already wrought. Reason becomes the resource of first and last resort. We expect everything to be done by reason and we lose the faculties, the capacities, and inclination necessary to perform other cognitive operations such as reconnaissance, characterization, description, apperception.

The rationalist aesthetic enables us (you and me) to believe that we are rationally choosing what should be done. Whether, in any given instance, we are "choosing" and whether anything will be "done" as a result of our choice is often highly questionable. What is not questionable, however, is that this rationalist aesthetic effectively shapes our thought, our law, indeed, our very lives.

The Shallowness Problem

The rationalist aesthetic reduces understandings and capacities to mere "positions," "methods," "theories" that one is supposed to choose. This is no small thing. To the extent intellectual and social culture is screened and formated in the image of the rationalist aesthetic, we lose depth, dimension, and contrast. Ultimately, cultural and individual memory are erased. The books, the archives, the lost worlds may remain in the library. But they are of no use: we have lost the ability to read them. Ultimately, our mode of thought itself becomes shallow. And when this is the case, there is not a thing that thought, as such, can do about it: shallow in/shallow out. The rationalist aesthetic becomes the frame within which thought occurs. The more it succeeds, the more it obliterates everything else.

In the law schools, this loss has already largely occurred. If one peruses the voluminous printed masses of legal thought today, the recurrent question seems to be "What should the law do about this or that?" Legal thinkers and actors are so enthralled by the prospect of constructing reasoned arguments to "choose" for or against this or that position, that they seem to do little else. Now, the single-minded pursuit of this question might well be warranted if all the other questions had already been answered. Questions like:

> Is there a discernible legal method?
> How and why is it authoritative?
> What are the limits of law and legality?
> How does law produce its effects?
> What is law?
> (and so on).

The truth of the matter, however, is that there are no generally accepted (or even generally acceptable) answers to any of these questions. But even without the foggiest notion of what the answers to these questions might look like, legal thinkers simulate the behavior of legal actors: legal thinkers propose solution upon solution and advocate prescription upon prescription.

This is the way legal thinkers and actors have been framed. This is their orientation. To be legally trained is to undergo a serious reduction of one's cognitive possibilities. This is not a remediable aspect of law as we know it. On the contrary, it is a constitutive aspect of law as we know it. The reduced cognitive possibilities are precisely how law becomes law: certain thoughts become simply unthinkable. The residue that remains after the cognitive reduction is what we call "law."[1]

One thinks of the shallowness problem as particularly troublesome for intellectuals. Shallowness is particularly troublesome for those intellectuals whose ambition it is to perfect thinking. But there is a sense in which this problem can have much more significant and wider implications. Indeed, to the extent that the shallowness problem affects a discipline that has a social and political dimension (namely, law), the shallowness problem becomes a problem for everyone. The problem is that as shallow forms of thought become the organizational frame of daily life, language, entertainment, the arts, it is life itself that becomes shallow. With the shallowness problem, most of that which might be interesting to think or rewarding to live remains beyond reach.

The Excessive Construction of Everything

Once reason becomes the rule of reason—once other forms of thought, perception, understanding are displaced—reason is left free to build on itself. Whether as critical reflexivity or as rational frame construction, this is not an auspicious development. In the law schools and in the courts, we now see the rule of reason madly building on itself.

Reason becomes the moniker, the vehicle, the excuse, and the justification for the construction of endless legal mazes, the piling on of endless legal distinctions, the excruciating refinement of ever more precise doctrinal taxonomies. Legal actors and thinkers become prisoners of the small frame—captives of small thinking. They construct little doctrines to modify other little doctrines. Indeed, American legal thinkers are fascinated with the most tedious and ephemeral details of appellate court opinions or statutory language. They spend their time recovering endless bits of legal data so as to integrate them into extremely massive and intricate, but ephemeral and unenlightening, compendiums and commentaries stating what the law is.

Reason/Not

What is called reason these days is very often not. Very often "reason" is little more than a pleasant name for faith, dogma, prejudice, and company. This rather sinister development comes from precisely the partisans of reason—those who claim to be its champions. What is perhaps most sinister is that the assault is not noticed much.

This enchantment of reason is a latent possibility of the identity of reason itself. Reason is typically deployed to help select, monitor, and replace beliefs. Given this exalted mission, it is not surprising if the role of reason should metamorphose into the rule of reason.

But law has much to do with the enchantment of reason as well. Law, such as we know it, is an opportunistic enterprise. This opportunism is a source of its virtue and of its vice. Law will use (and use up) the materials at hand to fortify and extend its dominion. In this endeavor, the legal mode of thought knows no scruples and no self-restraint. For law, reason is just another tool, just another cultural resource, just another set of techniques available to do law's work. Given the chance, law will appropriate, consume, and corrupt any cultural or intellectual resource—including reason itself.

Reason is unstable. Law is not benign. This is not a great combination. When reason runs out, but continues to rule, we get precisely what we see all around us—the excessive construction of a pervasively shallow form of life.

Notes

Introduction

1 E. A. Poe, "The Purloined Letter" (1845), reprinted in *Tales of Edgar Allan Poe* (1991).
2 For one example, see Jacques Lacan, "The Purloined Letter," in *The Seminar of Jacques Lacan*, bk. 2, *The Ego in Freud's Theory and in the Technique of Psychoanalysis, 1954–1955*, 191–205 (Jacques-Alain Miller ed., Sylvana Tomaselli trans., 1988).
3 Poe, supra note 1 at 225.
4 Id. at 232 (emphasis in the original).
5 Stanley Fish, "Critical Self-Consciousness," in *Doing What Comes Naturally: Change, Rhetoric, and the Practice of Theory in Literary and Legal Studies* (1989).
6 This is a point developed by Lacan. See supra note 2.
7 For an illustration of this tendency in the context of legal rights, see P. Schlag, "Rights in the Postmodern Condition," in *Legal Rights: Historical and Philosophical Perspectives* 263–82 (A. Sarat & T. R. Kearns eds., 1996).
8 For one argument along these lines, see P. Schlag, "Law and Phrenology," 110 *Harv. L. Rev.* 877 (1977).

1 Faith in the Power of Reason

1 M. Heidegger, *An Introduction to Metaphysics* 7 (1959).
2 J. H. Schlegel, *American Legal Realism and Empirical Social Science* 50 (1995).
3 "America's Best Graduate Schools," 118 *U.S. News & World Rep.*, Mar. 20, 1995, at 84.
4 Marbury v. Madison, 5 U.S. (Cranch) 137, 163 (1803).
5 J. Raz, *The Authority of Law: Essays on Law and Morality* 212–19 (1979); L. Fuller, *The Morality of Law* (1964). See also G. P. Fletcher, *Basic Concepts of Legal Thought* 11–27 (1996).
6 O. Fiss, "The Death of the Law?," 72 *Cornell L. Rev.* 1, 9 (1986).
7 Raz, supra note 5 at 3.
8 Id.
9 This is not unlike the unifying, systematizing role accorded to reason by Kant. I. Kant, *Critique of Pure Reason* 534–38 (1965).
10 R. Nagel, "The Formulaic Constitution," 84 *Mich. L. Rev.* 165 (1985).
11 The term originates with Rebecca French. For elaboration, see R. R. French, *The Golden Yoke* (1994).
12 I am grateful to Rebecca French for suggesting this image.
13 In table 1, "reason" can be read as the key categorical dyad. That, of course, is not entirely apt since such an understanding, in effect, already enshrines a "central command" view of reason; in such an understanding, reason is already represented as regulating

the content of the other dyads. The table, however, could be read more holistically with the central command/big tent dyad as just another dyad circulating with other dyads in the big tent. On this latter understanding, one would understand the central command/big tent dyad as occurring recursively within the other dyads, just as all the other dyads are occurring recursively within all the others.

14 This line of thought is very much indebted to Duncan Kennedy's pathbreaking work on "rules and standards." Duncan Kennedy, "Form and Substance in Private Law Adjudication," 89 *Harv. L. Rev.* 1685, 1687–1701 (1976). For other discussions, see P. Schlag, "Rules and Standards," 33 *UCLA L. Rev.* 379 (1985); M. Kelman, *A Guide to Critical Legal Studies* 15–63 (1987); F. Schauer, *Playing by the Rules* (1991); Kathleen M. Sullivan, "The Supreme Court, 1991 Term — Foreword: The Justices of Rules and Standards," 106 *Harv. L. Rev.* 22, 62–67 (1992).

2   *When Reason Runs Out*

1 S. Fish, "Fraught with Death: Skepticism, Progressivism, and the First Amendment," 64 *U. Colo. L. Rev.* 1061, 1066 (1993).

2 And indeed, much of the appeal of balancing came from the hope that the substantive emptiness of balancing would prompt an articulation of substantive reasons. P. Schlag, "An Attack on Categorical Approaches to Freedom of Speech," 30 *UCLA L. Rev.* 671, 731–39 (1983).

3 For elaboration, see P. Schlag, "Clerks in the Maze," in P. F. Campos, P. Schlag, & S. D. Smith, *Against the Law* 218 (1996).

4 A. R. Amar, "The Case of the Missing Amendments: *R.A.V. v. City of St. Paul*," 106 *Harv. L. Rev.* 124, 125 (1991).

5 R. Dworkin, *Law's Empire* 398. (1986).

6 H. L. A. Hart, *The Concept of Law* 94 (1961).

7 Id. at 98–107.

8 The phrase is borrowed from Leon Lipson who is rumored to have said, "Anything you can do, I can do meta."

9 Indeed, it puts one in mind of the celebrated constitutional law case of *Marbury v. Madison* where Chief Justice Marshall argued that to allow Congress to decide on the constitutionality of its own legislative actions would be to render the rule of law futile. Marbury v. Madison, 5 U.S. (Cranch) 137 (1803).

Marshall seems to be quite cognizant that to defer to Congress in this case would mean allowing Congress to be a judge in its own case. What he seems to overlook — indeed repeatedly so — is that for him to act on his interpretations of the Constitution and the congressional statute is in effect to be a judge in his own case: It is to rule on what the Constitution authorizes him and his court to do.

This, of course, is nothing other than an early, much celebrated and, dare one say, foundational? use of the Noble Scam.

10 J. Rawls, *Political Liberalism* 243 n.32 (1993) (emphasis added). For criticism of Rawls's "reasoning" here, see R. Posner, *Overcoming Law* 189–90 (1995). See also P. Campos, "Secular Fundamentalism," 94 *Colum. L. Rev.* 1814 (1994).

3   *The Arguments for Reason*

1   R. Nozick, *The Nature of Rationality* 6 (1993).
2   I. Kant, *Critique of Pure Reason* 534–38 (1965).
3   C. Sunstein, "Incommensurability and Valuation in Law," 92 *Mich. L. Rev.* 779, 810 (1994).
4   The possibilities include:
      A discussion of the relative domains or competencies of pluralism and monism
      An exploration of their relative virtues and vices
      A discussion of the extent to which they truly are incompatible
      A description of how each might characterize the other
      A description of how reason might go about identifying actual instances of radical incommensurability as distinguished from weak incommensurability
      A critique (an inquiry into the conditions of possibility) of pluralism and monism
      A discussion of the cognitive indicia and responses to pluralism and monism
      [And so on].
5   Prior to Professor Sunstein's essay, there was, of course, Steven Winter's article on incommensurability, entitled "Indeterminacy and Incommensurability in Constitutional Law," 78 *Cal. L. Rev.* 1441 (1990). Professor Sunstein seems to have been unaware of this earlier work.
6   Sunstein, supra note 3 at 810 (emphasis added).
7   I am indebted to Paul Campos for the joke.
8   P. Feyerabend, *Farewell to Reason* 116 (1987).
9   The point is elaborated in Kant, supra note 2 at 538.
10   Feyerabend, supra note 8 at 90–127.
11   Sunstein, supra note 3 at 811 n.113.
12   In the traditional image (from Plato to Freud), it is the disproportionate development of the appetites.
13   J. Raz, *Authority of Law: Essays on Law and Morality* 219 (1979).
14   H. Wechsler, "Neutral Principles," 73 *Harv. L. Rev.* 9 (1959); L. Fuller, *The Morality of Law* (1964).
15   For one recent example of this argument, see M. Nussbaum, "Commentary: Skepticism About Practical Reason in Literature and the Law," 107 *Harv. L. Rev.* 714, 741 (1994).
16   Id. at 715.
17   Id. at 741.
18   The mistake is sufficiently common that it bears quoting Derrida in full:
      What differs? Who differs? What is *différance*? If we answered these questions before examining them as questions, before turning them back on themselves, and before suspecting their very form, including what seems most natural and necessary about them, we would immediately fall back into what we have just disengaged ourselves from. In effect, if we accepted the form of the question, in its meaning and its syntax ("what is?" "who is?" "who is it that?") we would have to conclude that *différance* has been derived, has happened, is to be mastered and governed on the basis of the point of a present being, which itself could be some thing, a form, a state, a power in the world to which all kinds of names might be given, a *what*, or a present being as a *subject*, a *who*. . . .

Now if we refer once again, to semiological difference, of what does Saussure, in particular, remind us? That "language [which only consists of differences] is not a function of the speaking subject." This implies that the subject (in its identity with itself, or eventually in its consciousness of its identity with itself, its self-consciousness) is inscribed in language, is a "function" of language, becomes a *speaking* subject only by making its speech conform—even in so-called "creation," or in so-called "transgression"—to the system of the rules of language as a system of differences, or at very least by conforming to the general law of *différance*.

J. Derrida, *Margins of Philosophy* 14–15 (Allan Bass trans., 1982) (emphasis in the original). See also " 'Eating Well' or the Calculation of the Subject," in J. Derrida, *Points . . . Interviews* 1974–1994, 255 (Elisabeth Weber ed., Peggy Kamuf trans., 1995).

19 For further elaboration, see Pierre Schlag, " 'Le Hors de Texte—C'est Moi': The Politics of Form and the Domestication of Deconstruction," 11 *Cardozo L. Rev.* 1631 (1990).

20 Nussbaum, supra note 15 at 718–19.

21 Feyerabend, supra note 8 at 99–100.

22 B. Pascal, *Pensées,* sec. 233 (1670).

23 Id.

24 S. Žižek, "How Did Marx Invent the Symptom?" in *Mapping Ideology* 320 (1994).

25 S. Sherry, "The Sleep of Reason," 84 *Georgetown L.J.* 453, 472–84 (1996).

26 B. Ackerman, *We The People* 313 (1991).

27 Sherry, supra note 25 at 477–78.

28 J. Beale, *Treatise on the Conflict of Laws* 39 (2d ed. 1935).

29 P. Soper, "Dworkin's Domain," 100 *Harv. L. Rev.* 1166, 1173 (1987) (Book Review).

30 For general discussion, see J. Habermas, "Discourse Ethics: Notes on a Program of Philosophical Justification," in *The Communicative Ethics Controversy* 60 (S. Benhabib & F. Dallmayr eds., 1990).

31 Habermas does not quite agree with this point, but comes quite close. Id. at 96–106.

32 On the contrary, for Pascal, man is miserable without God. Pascal, supra note 22, sec. 72.

33 See Sherry, supra note 25 at 474.

34 See generally S. D. Smith, "Nonsense and Natural Law," in P. F. Campos, P. Schlag, & S. D. Smith, *Against the Law* 100 (1996).

4 Predicaments of Reason

1 I. Kant, Critique of Pure Reason 573 (1965).

2 J. Searle, *The Construction of Social Reality* 178 (1995).

3 H. Schnadelbach, "Remarks About Rationality and Language," in *The Communicative Ethics Controversy* 270, 271 (S. Benhabib & F. Dallmayr eds., 1990).

4 For discussion, see J. Habermas, "Discourse Ethics: Notes on a Program of Philosophical Justification," in Benhabib & Dallmayr eds., supra note 3 at 76–78; K. O. Appel, "Is the Ethics of the Ideal Communications Community a Utopia? On the Relationship Between Ethics, Utopia and the Critique of Utopia," in id. at 42–44; H. Albert, Treatise on Critical Reason 16–21 (1985).

5 Belief, of course, is hardly a terminus or a final ground. On the contrary, belief here is a shorthand for a referent that may itself dissolve into habit, convention, power (and so on). But for now, we go no further than belief.

6 P. Schlag, "Law and Phrenology," 110 *Harv. L. Rev.* 877 (1997).

7 S. Fish, *Doing What Comes Naturally: Change, Rhetoric, and the Practice of Theory in Literary and Legal Studies* (1989).

8 Id.

9 See, e.g., C. Sunstein, "Incommensurability and Valuation in Law," 92 *Mich. L. Rev.* 779, at 810 (asserting that radical incommensurability is rare because people who face incommensurability think "*rightly,* that their judgments are based on reasons").

10 R. Nozick, *The Nature of Rationality* 71–72 (1993); R. Posner, *Overcoming Law* 177 (1995).

11 Kant, supra note 1 at 593.

12 Nozick, supra note 10.

13 Id. at 532. ("[H]uman reason has a natural tendency to transgress these limits, and . . . [to] produce what through a mere illusion is none the less irresistible, and the harmful influence of which we can barely succeed in neutralizing even by means of the severest criticism.")

14 J. Dewey, *Human Nature and Conduct* 72 (1957).

15 H. M. Hart Jr., "The Supreme Court 1958 Term—Foreword: The Time Chart of the Justices," 73 *Colum L. Rev.* 84, 17–8 (1959).

16 F. W. Nietzsche, *Beyond Good and Evil* 13 (1989).

17 H. G. Gadamer, *Truth and Method* 269 (1975).

18 M. Foucault, *The Order of Things* 297 (1970).

19 J. Derrida, "Afterword: Toward an Ethic of Discussion," in Limited Inc. III, 136 (Samuel Weber trans., 1988).

20 J. F. Lyotard, *The Differend* 32 (Georges Van Den Abbeele trans., 1990) (emphasis added).

21 G. Deleuze & F. Guattari, *What Is Philosophy?* 27 (1994).

22 Fish, supra note 7.

23 As Jacques Derrida's provocative slogan puts it, "There is nothing outside the text." J. Derrida, *Of Grammatology* 154, 159 (1976). It is important, of course, to understand that for Derrida "text" does not mean what it often means in law or legal thought or American analytical philosophy.

24 B. Allen, *Truth in Philosophy* 106 (1993).

25 We do not usually think *self-consciously* of reason in the metaphors of maps, movement, travel—but in point in fact, the metaphors are apt. When one thinks of deductive or inductive reason, it seems clear that we are using reason *to get from a place we already are to a new place.* The metaphors seem even more apt if we are talking about instrumental reason or practical reason. In that case, reason is aimed at *arriving at* a particular solution.

26 I follow here the suggestions of Paul Diesing in suggesting that reason is both creativity and order. P. Diesing, *Reason in Society: Five Types of Decisions and Their Social Conditions* 242–43 (1962).

27 The point here is perhaps best summarized by Kenneth Burke, who points that social orders are afflicted with what he calls "occupational psychosis." In hunting societies, the categories and grammar of the hunt are likely to be used to name and describe all manner of other human activities, including, for instance, courtship or marriage or the like. The form of thinking (and perforce, "reason") within such a society would also be marked out in the categories and grammar of the hunt. The same sort of transposition

from the material and social to the ideational and symbolic would also take place in industrial and postindustrial societies. In terms of American society, one would expect reason (at least, in academic circles) to mimic the forms of the commodity economy, science, and technology. K. Burke, *Permanence and Change: An Anatomy of Purpose* 37–40 (1984).

28 Nozick, supra note 10 at 123.

29 Id. at 175–76.

30 Id. at 98.

31 S. Toulmin, *Human Understanding: The Collective Use and Evolution of Concepts* 503 (1972).

32 Id. at 484.

33 Id. at 500 (emphasis added).

34 Fish, supra note 7 at 437.

35 Id. at 440.

36 Id.

37 M. J. Radin, "The Pragmatist and the Feminist," 63 *S. Cal. L. Rev.* 1699 (1990).

38 Compare M. Minow & E. V. Spelman, "In Context," 63 *S. Cal. L. Rev.* 1597 (1990), with M. J. Radin, supra note 36 at 1699, with D. Farber, "Legal Pragmatism and the Constitution," 72 *Minn. L. Rev.* 1331 (1988), with S. Sherry, "The Ninth Amendment: Righting an Unwritten Constitution," 64 *U. Chi.-Kent L. Rev.* 1001, 1013 (1989), with T. Grey, "Hear the Other Side: Wallace Stevens and Pragmatist Legal Theory," 63 *S. Cal. L. Rev.* 1569, 1571–72 (1990), with J. W. Singer, "The Player and the Cards: Nihilism and Legal Theory," 94 *Yale L.J.* 1 (1984).

39 R. Barthes, *Mythologies* 153 (1993).

40 W. James, *Pragmatism* 26 (1975); Grey, supra note 38 at 1583.

41 These binaries destined for pragmatic "mediation" or "oscillation" are drawn from Radin, supra note 37 at 1707–15 and Grey, supra note 38 at 1571–72.

42 S. Smith, "The Pursuit of Pragmatism," 100 *Yale L.J.* 409 (1990).

43 T. S. Eliot, "Francis Herbert Bradley," in *Selected Prose of T. S. Eliot* 204 (Frank Kermode ed., 1975).

44 M. J. Radin, "Lacking a Transformative Social Theory: A Response," 45 *Stan. L. Rev.* 409, 424 (1993) (emphasis added).

45 See L. Wittgenstein, *On Certainty* § 359 (D. Paul & G. E. M. Anscombe trans., 1969).

46 D. Patterson, "Wittgenstein and Constitutional Theory," 72 *Tex. L. Rev.* 1837, 1841 (1994).

47 Dennis Patterson, a prominent neo-Wittgensteinian puts it this way: "It is not a matter of 'applying' Wittgenstein (would that it were so easy!) as much as approaching problems having been informed by Wittgenstein's insights and approaches." Id. at 1843.

48 And indeed, some neo-Wittgensteinians, go quite some distance in acknowledging as much. See, e.g., Patterson, supra note 45. As Professor Linda Meyer puts it: "Whether one reads Wittgenstein as a pragmatist, a skeptic, or a nonskeptic clearing away false philosophical problems, it seems clear that to ask, as the indeterminacy theorists do, whether law is indeterminate on a global level is to fall into one of the philosophical mistakes Wittgenstein tries to correct." L. Meyer, "When Reasonable Minds Differ," 71 *N.Y.U.L. Rev.* 1467, 1476–77 (1996).

49 Testimony of George Priest (September 25, 1987) as printed in Hearings Before the

Committee on the Judiciary on the Nomination of Robert H. Bork to Be Associate Justice of the Supreme Court of the United States, 100th Cong., 1st Sess. 2439, 2440–41 (1989).

50 R. Posner, *Overcoming Law,* 188 (1995).

51 C. Sunstein, "Propter Honoris Respectum: Rights and Their Critics," 70 *Notre Dame L. Rev.* 727, 729 (1995) (emphasis added).

5 Divine Deceptions

1   F. Nietzsche, *Twilight of the Idols* 47 (1990).

2   L. Feuerbach, *The Essence of Christianity* 22 (1989).

3   K. Burke, A Rhetoric of Motives 298–301 (1969).

4   P. Schlag, "This Could Be Your Culture—Junk Speech in a Time of Decadence," 109 *Harv. L. Rev.* 1801 (1996) (book review).

5   R. K. Collins & D. Skover, *Death of Discourse* (1996).

6   M. Redish, "The Value of Free Speech," 130 *U. Pa. L. Rev.* 678 (1982).

7   J. B. White, *Heracles' Bow: Essays on the Rhetoric and Poetics of Law* (1985).

8   J. B. White, *Acts of Hope Creating Authority in Literature, Law and Politics* 178 (1994).

9   For recent examples of sophisticated attempts at "synthesis," see E. L. Rubin, "The New Legal Process, The Synthesis of Discourse, and the Microanalysis of Institutions," 109 *Harv. L. Rev.* 1393 (1996); T. Grey, "Hear the Other Side: Wallace Stevens and Pragmatist Legal Theory," 63 *S. Cal. L. Rev.* 1569 (1990).

10 M. Kelman, "Interpretive Construction in the Substantive Criminal Law," 33 *Stan. L. Rev.* 591 (1981).

11 Who could be cited here? Who couldn't?

12 C. Sunstein, *Legal Reasoning and Political Conflict* 7 (1996) (emphasis added).

13 See generally P. Schlag, "The Problem of the Subject," 69 *Tex. L. Rev.* 1627 (1991).

14 For elaboration, see P. Schlag, "Hiding the Ball," 71 *N.Y.U.L. Rev.* 1681 (1996).

15 For a sophisticated understanding of the metaphorical enframing of law, laws, and legal artifacts, see the work of Steven Winter who elaborates on Lakoff and Johnson. See, e.g., S. Winter, "Indeterminacy and Incommensurability in Constitutional Law," 78 *Calif. L. Rev.* 1441 (1990).

16 This is, by no means, a rhetorical question. It is, however, beyond the purview of the present discussion.

17 Hart, *The Concept of Law* (1961).

18 If an entire community believes in magic (the same magic) then magic has, within limits, a certain efficacy. We could call this *placebo jurisprudence.*

19 S. D. Smith, "Law Without Mind," 88 *Mich. L. Rev.* 104 (1990).

20 Schlag, supra note 4.

21 F. Cohen, "Transcendental Nonsense and the Functional Approach," 35 *Colum. L. Rev.* 809 (1935).

22 For a variety of critical legal studies reification-critiques, see K. Klare, "Law-Making as Praxis," 40 *Telos* 123 (1979); P. Gabel, "Reification in Legal Reasoning," 3 *Res. Law & Soc.* 25 (1980); J. Boyle, "The Politics of Reason: Critical Legal Theory and Local Social Thought," 133 *U. Pa. L. Rev.* 685 (1986); R. W. Gordon, "Unfreezing Legal Reality: Critical Approaches to Law," 15 *Fl. St. U. L. Rev.* 195 (1987).

23 To be clear, I am not here advancing some sort of extrasocial, dehistoricized notion of what law is or must be. I am simply making a small situated observation of the character of American law. It seems to me that the objectivist and subjectivist aesthetic are so wrapped up in what we take American law to be, that if they were to disappear we would be dealing with a very different kind of law—one that might not look very much like law from our present understanding of what law is. We can, of course, develop different understandings of what law is, but they will be just that: different understandings. And it is not because we will attach the sign "l-a-w" to them that we will therefore think of them as "law." Word magic only gets you so far.

24 Schlag, supra note 13 at 1642–44, 1654–56.

25 For an exploration of the lack of attention to the problem of the subject, see id.

26 Indeed, as Derrida cautions, "[T]he simple practice of language ceaselessly reinstates the new terrain on the oldest ground." J. Derrida, "The Ends of Man," in *Margins of Philosophy* 135 (A. Bass trans., 1982).

27 A. Kocourek, *Jural Relations* 234 (1927) (emphasis added).

28 S. D. Smith, "Radically Subversive Speech and the Authority of Law," 94 *Mich. L. Rev.* 348 (1995).

29 See generally Schlag, supra note 13.

30 The expression "legal cosmology" comes from Rebecca French's work on the Tibetan legal system. It is this idea that allows one to think about the constitutive aspects of a legal system—what kinds of things with what kinds of power and what kinds of meanings are provided by a legal system. This way of thinking allows the distantiation, the detachment from the legal system that is necessary to begin any understanding of what it is, means or does. See generally R. R. French, *The Golden Yoke* (1994).

31 P. Schlag, "Contradiction and Denial," 87 *Mich. L. Rev.* 1216 (1989).

32 Hart, supra note 17 at 88–91; R. Dworkin, *Law's Empire* 13–14 (1986).

33 P. Gewirtz, "On 'I Know It When I See It,'" 105 *Yale L.J.* 1023, 1046 (1996).

34 See P. Schlag, "Law as a Continuation of God by Other Means," 85 Cal. L. Rev. 427 (1997).

35 S. D. Smith, "Idolatry in Constitutional Interpretation," in P. F. Campos, P. Schlag & S. D. Smith, *Against the Law* (1996).

36 F. Michelman, "Review Essay: The Subject of Liberalism," 46 Stan. L. Rev. 1807 (1994).

37 See, e.g., P. Brest, "The Misconceived Quest for the Original Understanding," 60 B. U. L. Rev. 204 (1980).

38 Even when the reason of legislation is in question—for instance, when the legislation is being challenged on a variety of constitutional grounds—the very test used (means/ends analysis) is framed within this idealized image. The means/ends test (rational relation, strict scrutiny, etc.) is whether some reasoned (and normatively appealing) end is appropriately related to the means adopted.

39 Now, of course, sometimes despite this aesthetic rationalization of law, a particular law can nonetheless be seen to be irrational—for instance, failing a constitutional means/ends test, or inconsistent with sound social policy, or based on archaic assumptions. But that is neither here nor there. The point remains that specific laws (statutes, doctrines, and so on) are always already perceived, apprehended, and expressed within a frame that casts law, as well as the particular law in question, within the aesthetics, the idioms, and the image of reason.

40   F. Nietzsche, *Will to Power* § 550, 294–95 (1968).

41   The reference is to the jurisprudence of Ronald Dworkin. Dworkin, supra note 32.

42   H. M. Hart Jr. & A. M. Sacks, *The Legal Process: Basic Problems in the Making and Application of Law* 1378 (W. N. Eskridge & P. P. Frickey eds., 1994).

43   On "situation sense," see K. Llewellyn, "Remarks on the Theory of Appellate Decision," 3 *Vand. L. Rev.* 395, 397 (1950); K. Llewellyn, *The Common Law Tradition: Deciding Appeals* 121 (1960).

44   K. L. Karst, "The Pursuit of Manhood and the Desegregation of the Armed Forces," 38 *UCLA L. Rev.* 499, 563 (1991).

45   Dworkin, *Taking Rights Seriously* (1977).

46   Thurman Arnold, "Criminal Attempts—The Rise and Fall of an Abstraction," 40 *Yale L.J.* 53, 57–58 (1931), as quoted in L. Kalman, *The Strange Career of Legal Liberalism* 251 (1996).

47   For a thoroughgoing exploration and defense of analogical and abductive thinking, see S. Brewer, "Exemplary Reasoning: Semantics, Pragmatics, and the Rational Force of Legal Argument by Analogy," 109 *Harv. L. Rev.* 923 (1996).

48   I do not mean to imply any strict separation between these various kinds of formation. I do want to suggest, however, that the establishment of facts as facts stems from different kinds of sources and has different kinds of epistemological groundings (or lack thereof). I cannot elaborate here the very difficult issues posed by all this. But the key point here remains a simple one: Facts are not some independent domain exempt from the general and the abstract. Rather, facts are simply particular concatenations of the forces that feature within the general and the abstract.

6   The Legal Self

1   M. Heidegger, "Plato's Doctrine of Truth," in 8 *Philosophy in the Twentieth Century* 269–70 (W. Barrett & H. Aiken eds., 1962).

2   E. J. Weinrib, "Legal Formalism: On the Immanent Rationality of Law," 97 *Yale L.J.* 949 (1988).

3   According to Tom Grey, "[T]he distinctive feature of recent reinterpretations of pragmatism is . . . the idea that thought is essentially embedded in a context of social practice." T. C. Grey, "Holmes and Legal Pragmatism," 41 *Stan. L. Rev.* 787, 798 (1989).

4   S. Sherry, "The Sleep of Reason," 84 *Georgetown L.J.* 453, 477 (1996).

5   Id. at 473 (emphasis added).

6   Id. (citing C. W. Collier, "Intellectual Authority and Institutional Authority," 35 *Inquiry* 145, 165 (1992).

7   Id. at 484.

8   Id.

9   Professor Anthony Kronman who describes a life in the law as developing the faculty of "good judgment" in turn describes one of two components of good judgment as "detachment"—the ability to view and evaluate things from a detached perspective. The other component of good judgment is the capacity for empathy. Anthony Kronman, "Living in the Law," 54 *U. Chi. L. Rev.* 83 (1987).

10   Some schools of American jurisprudence—notably critical legal studies—have explored this problem at length. In cls thinking, there is a strong sense that law is itself insufficient to provide guidance as to what should be done. Guidance as to what

should be done must come from elsewhere—with that elsewhere usually identified as "politics." Cls thinkers, having taken note of this apparent radical freedom of the legal self, have opted to treat it as a nonproblem—indeed, as an opportunity.

11   The insight and the better part of this section come from F. Michelman, "Layers of Law," 1994 John Dewey Lecture in the Philosophy of Law, University of Minnesota Law School (Nov. 14, 1994).

12   A. A. Leff, "Unspeakable Ethics, Unnatural Law," 1979 *Duke L.J.* 1229.

13   In one sense, as Stanley Fish has argued, this is true of all disciplines. Blind spots are the price one pays for seeing something as opposed to seeing everything, which is to say nothing. Formalism is not avoidable. Nor would it be desirable to avoid all formalism. Indeed, a pure antiformalism must feel a lot like madness, like schizophrenia.

But still, what distinguishes law is that, in contrast to more vital academic disciplines, it seems to be committed to maintaining its blind spots and to cultivating its lack of curiosity. One of its animating desires is to avoid gaining knowledge and understanding—particularly about itself.

Epilogue

1   M. Kelman, *A Guide to Critical Legal Studies* 269 (1987).

Index

Abduction, 33
Academic discipline(s): pathologies of, 2–14
Ackerman, Bruce, 54
Aesthetic(s): legal, 98–111, 119–25. *See also* Monism; Objectivist aesthetic; Pluralism; Rationalist aesthetic; Spatial aesthetic; Subjectivist aesthetic; Time
Amar, Akhil, 33–36
American Law Institute, 26
Analytical philosophy: advances in, 10; aesthetics of, 13; as impoverished aesthetic, 49; as pre-critical, 56
Angels: and law, 17, 96. *See also* Magical thinking
Animism, 163. *See also* Magical thinking
Anti-formalism, 4, 67. *See also* Critical reflexivity; Neopragmatism
Arnold, Thurman, 123
Authority: of law, 106–12; of reason, 22–24
Autonomy of self. *See* Choice; Legal self

Balancing: as rhetorical device, 30–33, 38
Barthes, Roland, 84
Beale, Joseph, 55, 56
Belief: sources of, 22–24
Bourdieu, Pierre, 70, 77
Burke, Kenneth, 92

Choice: as aesthetic of the self, 127–35; as false empowerment, 133–35
Circularity: of academic disciplines, 10–11; of arguments for reason, 60–63; of law, 37; of law and fact, 124–25; and Pascal's wager, 57–58
Coherence: as disciplinary criterion, 6–7, 56; and neopragmatism, 83
Comprehensiveness: as disciplinary criterion, 6–7
Conscience, 112–14
Contexts of genesis, 63–79

Contextualism: as distorted by rationalism, 129–31; and neopragmatism, 81–86; and rule of law, 20–21
Conventionalism: as distorted by rationalism, 129–31
Court of reason, 25
Critical legal studies, 25, 67; and reification critique, 106
Critical reflexivity, 63–79, 144; as constructive, 65–66; and contexts of genesis, 63–79; pathology of, 67–68
Critics of reason: ethics of, 48–53

Deification: of reason, 92, 96–98
Deleuze, Gilles, and Guattari, Félix, 69–70
Disciplinary frames and thought, 3–11
Disciplinary grid(s), 3–11, 24; and nihilism, 142
Disciplinary police. *See* Police work
Disciplines, 1–14
Dissonance: of legal thinker, 17; of reason, 26–29
Doctrine(s): aesthetic of, 100–111, 119–24; as maze, 31–33. *See also* Legal artifact(s)
Dogma: of reason, 40–59
Dominance and submission: of legal self, 135–40
Dworkin, Ronald, 33–36, 68, 90, 91

Economic analysis. *See* Law and economics
Efficiency, 9
Eliot, T. S., 85
Enlightenment reason: as narrative, 131–35; and rejection of pluralism, 54–55, 131–35
External perspective, 36. *See also* Internal perspective

Facts: American obsession with, 124–25
Faith: as necessary to reason, 19–22; and superior status of reason, 58, 59
Farber, Dan, 84–85

Feuerbach, Ludwig, 44, 53
Feyerabend, Paul, 44, 53
Fish, Stanley, 8, 30, 70, 82, 89
Fiss, Owen, 21
Formalism. *See* Rationalist aesthetic
Formalization: drive toward, 13
Foucault, Michel, 69
Frame: disciplinary, 3–11. *See also* Rational
   frame construction
Freud, Sigmund, 64, 70
Fuller, Lon, 48

Gadamer, Hans Georg, 69–71, 77
Gewirtz, Paul, 113
God: death of, 20, 111–12
God term, 92
Grey, Tom, 84–86
Grid(s). *See* Disciplinary grid(s); Frame

Hart, H. L. A.: and infinite regress, 34–35;
   and secondary rules, 34, 35, 105,
Hart, Henry, 65–66
"Hercules," 33, 112. *See also* Dworkin
Hermeneutic circle. *See* Gadamer
Humanities, 5–13

Indeterminacy, 20
Infinite regress: and critical reflexivity, 64
Internal perspective, 112–14

Judge(s): as errant, 136; as state agents, 39
Judicial review, 35
Jurisprudence: as if, 108–11
Justice: and law, 8–9

Kalman, Laura, 123–24
Kant, Immanuel, 41, 60; and Dworkin, 68
Kocourek, Albert, 108
Kronman, Anthony, 19, 20

Language games, 86–89
Law: as cognitive impairment, 140; as cul-
   tural symptom, 14; as game, 34–36; as
   God substitute, 105–6; as intellectual
   discipline, 12, 13; as juristic science, 26;
   as nihilism, 142; as proliferating, 14
Law and economics, 94
Law and literature, 94
Leff, Arthur, 138
Legal analysis: and critical reflexivity,
   65–66; and legal tastes, 31–36

Legal artifacts: aesthetic of, 100–111,
   119–24. *See also* Doctrines; Policies;
   Principles; Rules; Standards
Legal ontology: and death of God, 111–12.
   See also Ontology
Legal process, 65–67
Legal realists, 67; and reification critique,
   106–8
Legal reasoning: *See* Aesthetics; Legal
   artifacts
Legal self, 126–29; as abstraction, 126;
   as autonomous, 128–29; as construct
   of rationalism, 127–33; as hollow, 126;
   and objectivist aesthetic, 135–40; predicaments of, 138–40; and rationalist
   aesthetic, 128–35; and subjectivist aes-
   thetic, 135–40. *See also* Dominance and
   submission
Llewellyn, Karl: and situation sense, 120
Logic of search, 3–11
Lyotard, Jean François, 70

Magical thinking, 17, 108–12
Magic words, 22, 30–31
Marx, Karl, 64, 105
Metaphor. *See* Aesthetic(s); Objectivist
   aesthetic; Subjectivist aesthetic
Metaphysics: and authority of law, 107–
   12; of law, 98–115; and supernatural law,
   110–11
Methodology: critique of, 3–11
Minow, Martha, 84, 85
Monism, 42–47

Neopragmatism: as false modesty, 81–86;
   as form of sleep, 17
Nietzsche, Friedrich, 69–70, 92, 105–6,
   116–17
Nihilism, 142
Nozick, Robert, 130, 131
Nussbaum, Martha, 16, 46, 48–51, 78–79

Objectivist aesthetic, 98–111; and legal rea-
   soning, 119–22; and reification, 106; and
   rule of law virtues, 100
Objectivity. *See* Objectivist aesthetic;
   Rationalism; Rule of law
Object of desire, 8–11
Object of inquiry, 4–6
Ontology: of law, 95–115

Partisans of reason: and arguments for reason, 40–59
Pascal's wager: and contemporary equivalents, 55–58; and reason, 53–58
Pathologies of reason, 1–2, 63–71, 116–19
Pluralism, 42–46
Poe, Edgar Allan, 2–17
Police work, 2–13
Policies: aesthetic of, 100–11, 119–24
Posner, Richard, 84–85
Powell, Thomas Reed, 121
Power: and construction of the self, 129–40; of reason, 19–29, 38–39
Pragmatism. See Neopragmatism
Priest, George, 90
Principles: aesthetic of, 100–11, 119–24
Procedures: disciplinary. See Methodology
Progressive corollary, 98–99
Progressive fallacy, 98–99
Progressive legal change, 11, 12
Pyrrho, 48–50

Radin, Margaret Jane, 83–86
Rational frame construction, 65–79; as destructive, 66–67; pathology of, 68
Rationalism, 127–40
Rationalist aesthetic, 127–35. See also Objectivist aesthetic; Subjectivist aesthetic
Rationality. See Critical reflexivity; Rational frame construction; Rationalism; Reason
Rationalization: of law, 115–19; of sources of belief, 40
Rawls, John, 37–38, 68
Raz, Joseph, 20
Realist(s). See Legal realists
Reason: as activity, 76–77; authority of, 22–24, 39; as belief, 58–59; betrayal of, 61; as big tent, 26–29; as central command, 26–29, 39; constitutive vulnerabilities of, 78–79; as dependent on belief, 61–63; and dread, 30, 34, 37; as exclusionary, 26–27; exhaustion of, 21; failure of arguments for, 60–79; as immanent, 24–29; as inclusionary, 23–29; as medium of control, 15–16, 24; as medium of pacification, 24; as medium of unification, 15; as modesty, 79–81; as network, 76–77; as path-creating, 76–77; in power, 38–39; as rationalization, 25, 26, 115–19; as subject to hijacking,

78–79; superior status of, 23–26; triumph of, 40–41; as violence, 53; as web of intelligibility, 59. See also Court of reason; Critical reflexivity; Critics of reason; Pathologies of reason; Rational frame construction; Rationalism; Rationalization; Rule of reason
Reasonable balance. See Balancing
Reasonableness. See Rationalization
Reflective equilibrium, 5, 68
Rigor(ous), 6, 7
Rule of law, 20–26
Rule of reason, 6, 7, 22–29, 40, 46–47; as avoidance of ethical life, 51–52. See also Reason: as big tent; as central command; as medium of control
Rule(s): aesthetic of, 100–111, 119–24

Sartre, Jean Paul, 70
Searle, John, 70, 77
Self. See Legal self
Sherry, Suzanna, 54–55, 131–35
Singer, Joseph, 84–85
Social sciences: as disciplines, 5–13
Socratic method, 121
Solipsism: academic, 10–11; disciplinary, 72–73; professional 5
Soper, Philip, 56
Spatial aesthetics, 3–10, 101–104, 119–22
Spelman, Elizabeth, 84
Spirituality: technocratization of, 93–94
Standards: aesthetic of, 100–111, 119–24
Subjectivist aesthetic, 98–111; and legal reasoning, 122–24; and rule of law virtues, 100
Subjectivity. See Subjectivist aesthetic
Submission. See Dominance
Sunstein, Cass, 16, 41–44, 46, 79, 96
Superstition. See Magical thinking; Magic words

Technocracy: spiritualization of, 93–94
Theoretical unmentionables, 112–14
Theory: as emulating law, 13; as lawlike, 13; as rationalization, 26
Thinking: as assimilation 74–75; as disjunction, 74–75; as displacement, 71–73, 75; as incompleteness, 73–75
Time: and aesthetics, 103
Toulmin, Stephen, 81–83

Unthought, 37, 69–77; as *différance,* 71; as hermeneutic circle, 71; as whatever, 71. *See also* Thinking

Violence: as aspect of law, 21

Wechsler, Herbert, 48
White, James Boyd, 94
Wittgenstein, Ludwig, 70, 86–89

Žižek, Slavoj, 54

2

Pierre Schlag is Byron White Professor of Constitutional
Law at the University of Colorado at Boulder.

Library of Congress Cataloging-in-Publication Data
Schlag, Pierre.
The enchantment of reason / Pierre Schlag.
Includes index.
ISBN 0-8223-2185-8 (hardcover : alk. paper).
— ISBN 0-8223-2214-5 (pbk. : alk. paper)
1. Law—United States—Methodology.   2. Law—United States—
Interpretation and construction.   I. Title.
KF380.S317   1998   349.73'01—DC21   97-32865 CIP